Jesus' Claims – Our Promises

JESUS' CLAIMS – OUR PROMISES

A Study of the
"I Am" Sayings of Jesus

Maxie Dunnam

THE UPPER ROOM
Nashville, Tennessee

Jesus' Claims – Our Promises

Scripture quotations not otherwise identified are from the Revised
Standard Version of the Bible, copyrighted 1946, 1952, and © 1971 by
the Division of Christian Education, National Council of the Churches of
Christ in the United States of America, and are used by permission.

Scripture quotations designated NEB are from *The New English Bible,*
© The Delegates of the Oxford University Press and the Syndics of the
Cambridge University Press 1961 and 1970, and are reprinted by
permission.

Scripture quotations designated KJV are from the King James Version of
the Bible.

Any scripture quotation designated AP is the author's paraphrase.

Selected lines from "The Conquerors" by Harry Kemp are reprinted by
permission of (Rose) Sunny Tasha and family.

"Because He Lives" by William J. and Gloria Gaither. © Copyright 1971
by William J. Gaither. All rights reserved. Used by permission of Gaither
Music Company.

Lines from "He Bought My Soul" by Stuart Hamblen. © Copyright 1948,
renewed 1976 by Hamblen Music: All rights reserved. Sheet music
available.

Excerpts from "The Minister" by Ted Schroeder first appeared in *alive
now!* (May/June 1980). Copyright Theodore W. Schroeder. Used by
permission of the author.

Book and Cover Design: Harriette Bateman
First Printing: January 1985 (10)
Second Printing: June 1985 (10)
Third Printing: April 1989 (5)
Fourth Printing: July 1990 (7)
Library of Congress Catalog Card Number: 84-051831
ISBN 0-8358-0502-6
Printed in the United States of America

Jesus' Claim Has Been My Promise

Have you not read that he who made them from
the beginning made them male and female, and
said, "For this reason a man shall leave his
father and mother and be joined to his wife, and
the two shall become one flesh"? So they are
no longer two but one flesh.
What therefore God has joined together,
let no man put asunder.

MATTHEW 19:4–6

*This book
is for my wife Jerry with whom Christ
has made me one.*

CONTENTS

PREFACE

The intent of this book is for personal devotional study and reflection, but also for group use. Originally The Upper Room editors and I projected it as a Lenten study, thus the decision to look at only seven of Jesus' claims. There are, of course, other equally important sayings of Jesus. Although the book is especially appropriate for Lent, I hope *Jesus' Claims—Our Promises* will yield inspiration for any season.

My prayer is that these chapters will open the holy of holies for you, providing a fresh and exciting revelation. May these claims of Jesus become promises upon which you lay hold for the new and living way Christ offers.

Grace and peace,
Maxie D. Dunnam

INTRODUCTION

In Mark's account of the crucifixion, after he speaks of Jesus' last anguished cry, he records this astonishing fact: "The veil of the temple was rent in twain from the top to the bottom" (15:38, KJV).

Just that; no more. Matthew elaborates a bit more, giving the impression that this ripping of the veil was a part of a great upheaval that rocked the earth (27:51–53).

In the Old Testament ceremonial symbolism, the veil stood for that which keeps God and humans apart. Behind the veil was the holy of holies, the dwelling place of God. To enter that place of the Presence meant instant death. One man, the high priest, could come into the Presence once a year on the great Day of Atonement, and then only after he was cleansed from all sin and made holy.

God was not to be looked upon by profane eyes, nor touched with profane hands, nor approached with profane steps. A barrier—the ominous veil designating the holy of holies—kept persons separated from God.

The Gospels' recording of the rending of the veil expressed a literal fact. The separating veil was torn in two from top to bottom. But, could that veil not be repaired and restored?

Here comes the deeper truth. The writer to the Hebrews says the veil has not only been rent, it has been done away with altogether. Another veil has replaced the old one through which every person may enter. This "veil" is Jesus' flesh. By this the writer means the sacrifice of Jesus Christ. By "the blood of Jesus," he says, we enter the holy place (Heb. 10:19–21). The new veil indicates not separation, but reconciliation, and everyone, not just an appointed person, may pass through it.

The writer to the Hebrews expresses the core truth of the gospel: "Now once in the end of the world hath [Christ] appeared to put away sin by the sacrifice of himself" (Heb. 9:26, KJV). There was a once and for all rending of the old veil and the establishment of a new. Yet, there is another truth that comes from this veil symbol.

Not only in his death, throughout his life Jesus was seeking to rend the veil, seeking to open up "the place of the Holy." And that is what this book is about.

In his great "I am" claims, Jesus is telling us who he is and who God is. He is inviting us to come into his presence, to gaze upon him, to listen to him, to touch him, to receive his love, to accept his forgiveness, to live in him.

Questions prepared by Marie Livingston Roy are provided for group use. Again, individuals can profit from these apart from group sharing, but I encourage you to invite some friends to share this study/reflection adventure with you. I am convinced that one of the most meaningful disciplines for spiritual growth is what we sometimes call "Christian conferencing"—deliberate sharing among Christians who are mutually committed to each other's spiritual well-being. One of the dynamics of the early Methodist classmeetings was "one loving heart setting another on fire." We need that, and it can happen if we are willing to share our journey with another. The best way to share the journey is by sharing a common content of study and reflection. I hope this book will be that resource for you.

1

I Am the Bread of Life

When they found him on the other side of the sea, they said to him, "Rabbi, when did you come here?" Jesus answered them, "Truly, truly, I say to you, you seek me, not because you saw signs, but because you ate your fill of the loaves. Do not labor for the food that perishes, but for the food which endures to eternal life, which the Son of man will give to you; for on him has God the Father set his seal." Then they said to him, "What must we do, to be doing the works of God?" Jesus answered them, "This is the work of God, that you believe in him whom he has sent." So they said to him, "Then what sign do you do, that we may see, and believe you? What work do you perform? Our fathers ate the manna in the wilderness; as it is written, 'He gave them bread from heaven to eat.'" Jesus then said to them, "Truly, truly, I say to you, it was not Moses who gave you the bread from heaven; my Father gives you the true bread from heaven. For the bread of God is that which comes down from heaven, and gives life to the world." They said to him, "Lord, give us this bread always."

Jesus said to them, "I am the bread of life; he

who comes to me shall not hunger, and he who believes in me shall never thirst."

—John 6:25–35

It is absurd to apologize for mystery. Lodge this thought solidly in your mind. We are embarking on a study that will tempt us to do just that—to apologize for mystery. There is mystery here, deep mystery in the great claims of Jesus. These claims often verge on the absurd even to the one who wants to believe. How absolutely absurd to the one who is seeking ardently not to believe.

There are some truths we do not appropriate simply by appealing to reason. Wonder and awe are not rational categories. Love cannot be dissected. Hope often defies what seems rational, and faith takes us beyond superficial reasonableness.

So, I will resist the temptation to apologize for mystery. I invite you to stand openly before Jesus and hear his words. Hear his words with your heart as well as your mind.

It is as we hear these "I am" claims of Jesus with heart and mind that they will become promises to us. These promises will become faith, hope, affirmation, direction; they will become *life*—that is the bottom line. Jesus said, "I came that they may have life, and have it abundantly" (John 10:10).

The first claim to which we listen is that astounding statement—"I am the bread of life." Let us begin to look and listen through a contemporary story.

Movie buffs may recall an Italian film of a few years ago entitled *La Dolce Vita*. The film opens with a helicopter flying slowly through the sky. It is not very high above the earth so you can see something dangling below it. In closer view, you make out that it is a life-sized statue of a man, arms outstretched, dressed in a robe, suspended in a kind of halter. The camera occasionally cuts out the helicopter, and it looks as though the man is flying by himself.

Men working in a field see the strange sight and begin to wave their hats and yell. One recognizes who it is a statue of and yells, "Hey, it's Jesus!" They begin to run after it and yell, but the helicopter moves on.

Then the copter comes to the edge of Rome and passes over a swimming pool on the roof of a building. Girls around the pool in their bikinis see the sight and also wave and shout. The young men flying the helicopter see the beautiful girls, circle back and hover over the pool, trying to communicate with the girls. Above the roar of the engines, they try to get the girls' telephone numbers, telling them they are taking the statue to the Vatican and will be happy to return as soon as their mission is over.

In *The Hungering Dark,* Frederick Buechner described the reaction of the audience in the little college town where he saw the film. The first reaction, he noted,

> was of course to laugh at the incongruity of the whole thing. There was the sacred statue dangling from the sky, on the one hand, and the profane young Italians and the bosomy young bathing beauties, on the other hand—the one made of stone, so remote, so out of place there in the sky on the end of its rope; the others made of flesh, so

bursting with life. Nobody in the audience was in any doubt as to which of the two came out ahead or at whose expense the laughter was. But then the helicopter continues on its way, and the great dome of St. Peter's looms up from below, and for the first time the camera starts to zoom in on the statue itself with its arms stretched out, until for a moment the screen is almost filled with just the bearded face of Christ—and at that moment there was no laughter at all in that theater full of students and their dates and paper cups full of buttery popcorn and La Dolce Vita college-style. Nobody laughed during that moment because there was something about that face, for a few seconds there on the screen, that made them be silent—the face hovering there in the sky and the outspread arms. For a moment, not very long to be sure, there was no sound, as if the face were their face somehow, their secret face that they had never seen before but that they knew belonged to them, or the face that they had never seen before but that they knew, if only for a moment, they belonged to.

Remember, it is absurd to apologize for mystery. And there is mystery here—in the way Jesus comes to us and in the way, when we are in the presence of Jesus, we must in our heart of hearts at least, be still and look and think and ask, "What have you to do with me?" "What must I do with you?"

This devotional study is an effort to focus our eyes on Jesus in a disciplined gaze, to deliberately position ourselves in relation to Jesus to receive his judgment and his grace.

We look specifically at some of Jesus' great "I am" claims, because with these Jesus provides us autobiographical vignettes; his words are a kind of self-portrait.

Jesus said to them, "I am the bread of life; he who comes to me shall not hunger, and he who believes in me shall never thirst."

Put this claim of Jesus in its immediate and its larger context. The question which evokes this claim of Jesus came from people who had been with Jesus on one side of the Sea of Galilee on the preceding day. There had been only one boat there, and the disciples had left without Jesus in that boat. Now, having come to where the disciples were, looking for Jesus, they found him but didn't know how or when he got there. "Rabbi, when did you come here?" they asked.

Jesus didn't answer the question they asked. Rather, he addressed the far deeper question—the question of hungering and thirsting for life. John connects this claim of Jesus with two miraculous events: the feeding of the five thousand and Jesus walking on the water. This explains that somewhat strange word of Jesus in verse 26: "You seek me, not because you saw signs, but because you ate your fill of the loaves."

Jesus had healed many and the crowds had seen the signs of his power. Jesus confronts these curious followers with the fact that their interest is not in who he is as the powerful son of God. They had been fed on the day before. "This is your motivation," Jesus said. "You ate your fill of the loaves." Then he made his point: "Do not labor for the food which perishes, but for the food which endures to eternal life, which the Son of man will give to you; for on him has God the Father set his seal."

Note one other dimension in the scriptural setting. Jesus' claim to be the bread of life is connected with that event in the wilderness when manna, "daily bread," was provided for Moses and the Israelites in their wilderness wandering. See it in verses 32-33:

> Jesus then said to them, "Truly, truly, I say to you, it was not Moses who gave you the bread from heaven; my Father gives you the true bread from heaven. For the bread of God is that which comes down from heaven, and gives life to the world."

Jesus knew that most, if not all the crowd, would know that story (faithful Jews that they were). "Now, don't be confused," he said. "What you experienced yesterday on the mountainside when the five thousand were fed—don't be confused about that. It was not Moses who gave you the bread of heaven. My Father gives you the true bread. For the bread of God is that which comes down from heaven and gives life to the world."

No wonder they said to him, "Lord, give us this bread always." Then came the claim: "I am the bread of life; he who comes to me shall not hunger, and he who believes in me shall never thirst."

It is absurd to apologize for mystery, so let's simply nail these truths down as the core of our learning today. First, *life depends on bread.* We can't live without being physically nourished. Second, *this physical bread is God-given.* Maltbie D. Babcock stated it clearly in *Thoughts for Everyday Living:*

Back of the loaf is the snowy flour,
Back of the flour, the mill;
Back of the mill are the wheat and the shower
And the sun and the Father's will.

Physical bread is God-given.

Third, *for all God's children to have this bread, we humans must corporately labor and share.* Augustine put this truth in one pithy sentence: "Without God, we cannot; without us, God will not." Leslie Weatherhead probes that lodestone of wisdom in *Over His Own Signature:*

Without God we cannot make a loaf. Without us God will not make a loaf. . . . We see, then, that a loaf of bread is a symbol of our utter dependence on God, of our utter dependence on bread, and in this form of society in which we live, of our utter dependence on those who make our bread for us. Those of us who live a very busy life might pause to remember that bread is so essential that unless some of us were farmers and millers all the time, all of us would have to be farmers and millers part of the time, for bread we must have.

Also, we need to remember that there are those who will not eat unless we provide them the bread to eat—that is, unless we provide the resources by which bread can be gotten to them.

We could rehearse the statistics: Millions of people starving in places with names that sound strange to us and which we can hardly pronounce, such as Bangladesh and Cameroon. The intensity of starvation may increase in one place this year and another the next. Then there is hunger, dehumanizing hunger, in the backyard of each of our cities and in almost every rural community.

Rehearsing statistics sensitizes us to the problem, but sometimes, God help us, our hearts grow calloused for hearing so much, or we harden ourselves in order not to feel the pain. As Christians we sometimes divert ourselves by focusing on our own situation, our own private and/or personal spirituality. We seek to assuage our guilt with promises of forgiveness. Jesus reminds us that that is not enough. Grace never comes cheaply, though it always comes. We cannot build our spiritual life on Psalm 23: "The Lord is my shepherd, there is nothing I shall want" (AP).

Nor can we escape social responsibility by immersing ourselves in so-called "personal religion." To claim that today the Lord heals inward blindness but not physical blindness, that the business of the church is to feed souls not bodies is a cop-out that will receive God's judgment of fire. Such claims would excuse us would-be followers of Christ to work signs and miracles, thus denying the call and the power of our Master. At the heart of the faith into which Jesus calls us is *compassion*. The fourteenth-century mystic, Meister Eckhart, said in one of his sermons:

> As long as you are more concerned for yourself than you are for people you have never seen, you are wrong and you cannot have even a momentary insight into the simple care of the soul.

That is a tough word—who can bear it? To pray for, much less to be more concerned for unknown people than for ourselves, is a grueling demand. Compassion does not come painlessly. Yet the truth remains: For all God's children to have bread, we humans must corporately labor and share.

Now a fourth truth: While life in its most elementary form depends on bread, bread only sustains life, it does not make life what God intended it to be. Parents, it is not enough simply to provide food and clothing for your children, not enough just to see that they get a good education. Husbands, wives, it is not enough that you share in the parenting process, not enough that you satisfy the sexual needs of your partners. For life to be more than staying alive there must be relationship: caring and sharing, tenderness, affection, giving as well as receiving love.

There must be shared values and commitments. I don't believe that people "fall in love"; they grow in love. Nor do people "fall out of love"; they cease loving because they cease growing in love.

Mohammed, the great prophet of Islam, expressed an important truth when he said, "If thou hast two loaves, sell one and buy lilies." He was right. We need more than bread. We need lilies. We need love and light, beauty and blessedness. The testimony of a successful businessman with an international reputation illustrates this very forcefully. A friend, Mark Trotter, heard the speech and shared it later in a sermon.

The businessman's work was so demanding of his time and his energies, he spent little time at home. Then he came to himself, and decided to do something about it.

His family consisted of three generations—his parents, he and his wife, and their children. Wanting to be sensitive to the needs of all the individuals in that large family, he brought them all together and asked each one of them if they would list the five human needs that they considered most important in their lives. Then they listened to each other. He said it was an enlightening exercise. He was surprised how much he learned. The temptation, especially for parents, is to project their desires on the children and assume that's what the children want. It's a temptation of husband and wife to hold images over their spouse's head and harbor resentment that the other person doesn't live up to that image. We don't really know who that other person is living in the house with us. It is very difficult for the other person to reveal who they are for fear of being rejected. Well, the businessman found a way to get at that. He had every member write down what they wanted—their needs—and then asked that every member of the family be supportive in helping that person become that.

The man said for him to do that with one of his sons was particularly difficult. His son's appearance and his lifestyle were just the opposite of what the parents had expected. The father was firmly ensconced in the conservative business community, he even looked like a successful business executive. His son wore the uniform of the counterculture. But they let him be, they knew who he really was, who he really wanted to be, and they waited patiently for him to find his own way.

He said that he came to know his son not only from these family conferences, but particularly from one special moment when he was attentive to his son. It happened some years earlier. They were in Indian Guides together. The father arranged his schedule to be in town on that particular day so that at least for a year he could spend some time with his son. As a service project the group would go to Rancho Los Amigos (Hospital) in Downey, California, and play bingo with the children in that hospital. And there was on the ward a spastic girl who had to be tied to her wheelchair, unable to control even the saliva flowing from her mouth. The boys were to go into that ward and select one of the children to play with. All the other boys quickly found partners, all of them avoiding the girl in the wheelchair, all except his son, who approached her with some hesitation, asked her if she would play. For an hour they played together. They talked, they laughed, and he wiped the saliva from her chin. The businessman concluded his speech with these words. He said, "No matter what my son does with his life now, I knew from that moment years ago, who he really is."

Even those who live with us are often strangers to us. If we have to work hard to stay sensitive to their needs for something other than bread, how much more effort must we put forth to live sensitive to needs of all people. And that brings us to a final truth.

Jesus said it: "Man shall not live by bread alone, but by every word that proceeds from the mouth of God" (Matt. 4:4). That was Jesus' answer to the devil when the devil tempted him to turn stones into bread.

For us, not only are we to live by the words of God as we find them in scripture, but by the Word of God which is Christ himself. Recently I heard Bishop Edward Tullis tell of a rewarding experience in a black congregation in Charleston, South Carolina:

After Sunday school, the Sunday school children come into the sanctuary and sit with the adults of the congregation who have already come in. The Superintendent of the Sunday school gets up and says, "Now, we're going to review the Sunday school lesson." This is before worship starts. Someone from each age-group tells the story of the Sunday school lesson.

That morning, a little twelve-year-old girl rose, and she said, "Our story this morning was about Enoch, and our text was 'Enoch walked with God, and was not, for God took him.'" She said, "You know, every morning when Enoch awakened, he prepared to go out and walk with God. Everyday, he'd walk with God in the community and in the various communities, seeking to do the things that needed to be done."

"But," she said, "one day, when they were out on a long walk, toward evening it became dusk, and God said to Enoch, 'Enoch, it's closer to my house tonight than it is to yours; why don't you just come and spend the night with me.'"

And she concluded, "Enoch and God had walked together so long and had come to love each other so much, that they just decided to stay in God's House."

It's a very simple story, but it is a profound truth that needs to find its way deeply into our hearts and minds. We walk with God by living with the words of God, but most of all, we live by *the* Word, Christ himself.

That brings us back to our primary focus, Jesus' claim, "I am the bread of life." The crowd was thinking, if not saying, "Wait a minute, it was Moses who gave our ancestors bread in the wilderness. Are you saying that you can do that too?"

Jesus said, "It wasn't Moses. It was God. God

gives light and life to the world. I am the bread of life, and he who comes to me will not hunger." The crowd said, "Lord, give us this bread always."

What do *you* say?

2

I Am the Good Shepherd

Jesus said, "I am the good shepherd. The good shepherd lays down his life for the sheep. He who is a hireling and not a shepherd, whose own the sheep are not, sees the wolf coming and leaves the sheep and flees; and the wolf snatches them and scatters them. He flees because he is a hireling and cares nothing for the sheep. I am the good shepherd; I know my own and my own know me, as the Father knows me and I know the Father; and I lay down my life for the sheep. And I have other sheep, that are not of this fold; I must bring them also, and they will heed my voice. So there shall be one flock, one shepherd. For this reason the Father loves me, because I lay down my life, that I may take it again. No one takes it from me, but I lay it down of my own accord. I have power to lay it down, and I have power to take it again; this charge I have received from my Father."

—John 10:11–18

In human relations it is often true that the more we know persons, the more we love them. This is true, but not because they become greater in our mind. As we come to know persons, we discover

29

their weaknesses: their faults and failures, their shames and shams. The amazing thing about Jesus is that the more we know about him, the greater he becomes and the more we love him.

It has been reported that Napoleon was once in the company of some clever skeptics who were discussing Jesus. They dismissed Jesus as a great man and nothing more. "Gentlemen," said Napoleon, "I know men, and Jesus Christ was more than a man." Richard Watson Gilder put it this way in "The Song of a Heathen":

> If Jesus Christ is man
>   And only a man,—I say
> That of all mankind I cleave to him,
>   And to him will I cleave alway.

> If Jesus Christ is a God—
>   And the only God,—I swear
> I will follow him through heaven and hell,
>   The earth, the sea, the air!

This is Christianity's ultimate paradox. Jesus is God and man. In this devotional study, we are seeking to know him by living with his great claims.

"I am the good shepherd," he says. But he goes even further. "All who came before me are thieves and robbers" (John 10:8).

This is no isolated, outrageous claim. We have already examined Jesus' claim to be the bread of life. As we will see, he makes other claims that are just as astounding: "I am the door" (John 10:1) and "I am the resurrection and the life" (John 11:25). If we thought he was a mere man, we would denounce him as a mad egotist. But the more we know him, the more we are convinced that this is God's own image—this is God. And when we see Jesus as the God who is the Good Shepherd, as the only God, we say again with the poet:

> I will follow him through heaven and hell,
> The earth, the sea, the air!

So, let's look; let's look long and longingly at this claim of Jesus: "I am the good shepherd." And even now, as you read, will you pray that this long and longing look will turn into love, an intense love that will fire your soul to follow this Good Shepherd wherever he leads. My guide for our long and longing look is simple: a *picture* of the Shepherd, the *priorities* of the Shepherd, and the *power* of the Shepherd.

First, a picture of the Shepherd. I remember vividly my first visit to the Holy Land. I'd never seen a large flock of sheep before. We didn't raise sheep in Mississippi. And I'd never seen a shepherd. I took more pictures of the shepherd and sheep than anything else on that trip. I'm sure it was not only the quaintness of the sight that attracted me, but the connection that was occurring in my consciousness between what I was actually seeing and all those images in the Bible of the Shepherd.

Seeing the shepherd moving across those barren, seemingly lifeless hills, alone, his sheep following after him, I realized that the shepherd is the only source of life for those sheep, that he will risk his life to protect them from robbers and wild animals, that he will spend himself to get them to pasture and water. The Psalms came alive for me:

The Lord is my shepherd, I shall not want.
—Psalm 23:1

We thy people, the flock of thy pasture, will give thanks to thee for ever.
—Psalm 79:13

Give ear, O Shepherd of Israel, thou who leadest Joseph like a flock!
—Psalm 80:1

When we get a picture of the shepherd in the life of Israel, we know why the prophet Isaiah would image the promised Messiah as a shepherd. "He will feed his flock like a shepherd, he will gather the lambs in his arms, he will carry them in his bosom, and gently lead those that are with young" (Isa. 40:11).

The picture becomes more vivid yet in the New Testament. Jesus said, "What do you think? If a man has a hundred sheep, and one of them has gone astray, does he not leave the ninety-nine on the mountains and go in search of the one that went astray?" (Matt. 18:12). And it was said of Jesus: "As he went ashore, he saw a great throng, and he had compassion on them, because they were like sheep without a shepherd" (Mark 6:34).

Jesus spoke tender and sad words, using this image: "Fear not, little flock, for it is your Father's good pleasure to give you the kingdom" (Luke 12:32). Peter sounded a similar note: "For you were straying like sheep, but have now returned to the Shepherd and Guardian of your souls" (1 Pet. 2:25).

The writer of the Hebrews provided us a great

benediction, using the shepherd image. "Now may the God of peace who brought again from the dead our Lord Jesus, the great shepherd of the sheep, by the blood of the eternal covenant, equip you with everything good that you may do his will" (Heb. 13:20–21).

The picture is clear, isn't it? Jesus is the shepherd who will risk his life to seek and save one straying sheep. He has pity upon the people because they are as sheep without a shepherd. His disciples are his little flock. He is the Great Shepherd of the souls of all people who has been brought again from the dead, having laid down his life for his sheep.

That's the picture. Look now at the priorities of the shepherd. The first priority of the shepherd is to *know his sheep*. What a claim Jesus makes: "I am the good shepherd; I know my own and my own know me." To get the full impact of that claim, we need to know something of sheep and shepherds in ancient Palestine.

In the villages, there were communal sheepfolds, to which the shepherds of the village brought their sheep at night. Out in the hills, far from the villages, there were also small enclosures made of stone to serve shepherds in the warm season when they did not return home for many weeks.

It is the large communal fold that Jesus is using as his image in John 10:1–5. At the entrance is the gatekeeper whose primary task is to keep guard and not to allow anyone but authorized shepherds to enter. Many flocks—some large, some small—are brought by their shepherds into the safety of the fold each night.

When morning comes and it is time for the shepherd to lead his sheep out to find pasture, how does he find his own amidst all the sheep in the fold? Strange as it may seem to us who know little or nothing about sheep, he calls them by name. He knows them, and they know his voice and they follow.

Get the full import of that. Christ the Good Shepherd knows me. Don't rush on in your reading. Pause, reflect, and get the full impact of this truth. Christ the Good Shepherd knows me! He knows my name. If we could appropriate that emotionally—really claim it as a truth for ourselves—it would radically transform our lives.

Think what it would do for our praying. Do you come hesitantly to prayer, not sure at all about making contact or how God will respond? When you pray, do you feel that you somehow must make a case and convince God that you have a right to be heard? Oh, my friend, take heart! Christ the Good Shepherd knows you by name, and you can come into his presence boldly.

My friend, Flora Wuellner, who has written a number of exceedingly helpful books on prayer, gives us a signal in *To Pray and to Grow*.

I joined an amateur choir several years ago. Once during rehearsal, the annoyed conductor told us to stop singing. "You're cheeping along like frightened orphans. Stop being apologetic. Open your mouths and sing." So we sang. Our mistakes were frightful, but he knew he couldn't get anywhere with us until we gave him our voices, mistakes and all. So we sang with the boldness of his acceptance. And as time went on, we sang with another boldness. We sang with the boldness of those who were actually learning how to sing.

That would happen to our praying if we really accepted the fact that the Good Shepherd knows us and calls us by name. Looking in another direction, think what that acceptance would do for the biggest problem most of us have—the problem of insecurity.

I doubt if there is a more ravaging problem than insecurity. Young people become victims of a crowd mentality—drugs, drinking, promiscuous sex—because they are insecure. They want to belong.

Unfortunately what begins so early may plague us forever. I recently counseled with a thirty-eight-year-old woman who is attractive, has a good personality, and whose husband loves her and provides economic security. Personal insecurity, however, often drives her to long sieges of depression. She developed slowly as a teenager, therefore she was not popular in high school. Her parents did not provide her the acceptance she needed, and her father, especially, had not given her a sense of value as a woman. She was midway through college before she began to date. All of that produced an insecurity that she has not yet conquered.

I see it all around—insecurity. At least 50 percent of the men I share with, either at a time of career change, economic difficulty, or midlife crisis, are battling the demon of insecurity.

In this claim of Jesus, "I am the good shepherd," and the implicit promise, he knows us by name, is some of best news I know! Our insecurity, whatever its source, can be overcome if we have the security of belonging to God.

I have a strong hunch, confirmed over and over again in my counseling, that most *continuing* insecurity is rooted in the lack of the assurance of belonging to God. Yet, whether rooted there or not, the strangling grip insecurity has in our lives can be loosened by the assurance that we belong to God.

As Christians, we know that we belong to God. This is the problem: We know it with our minds, but we don't accept it with our hearts. That is the reason I insisted at the beginning of chapter 1 that we hear with our hearts as well as with our minds. Listen to Jesus. Hear him. Believe him. Accept what he offers: "I am the good shepherd; I know my own, and my own know me."

Not only is *knowing* his own a priority of the good shepherd; to *nurture* his own is likewise a priority. The shepherd spends his life to nurture his sheep, plods the stark, barren land until he finds them pasture, the grass upon which his flock can feed.

One of Jesus' tenderest thoughts is recorded in Luke 12:32: "Fear not little flock, for it is your Father's good pleasure to give you the kingdom." That word follows Jesus' teaching about God's care for us.

Do not be anxious about your life, what you shall eat, nor about your body, what you shall put on. For life is more than food and the body more than clothing. Consider the ravens: they neither sow nor reap, they have neither storehouse nor barn, and yet God feeds them. Of how much more value are you than the birds!

—Luke 12:22–24

A teenager sent his girlfriend her first orchid with this note: "With all my love and most of my allowance." As the Good Shepherd, Jesus' word to us is, "With all my love and with all my resources." Knowing this, we Christians can make two bold assertions. First, Christ knows me and loves me just as I am. But that isn't all, nor is it enough. The second assertion is that Christ nurtures me—he changes me.

To stop with the first assertion—that Christ knows me and loves me just as I am—is to enter a static state that will become stale, boring, uncreative, unattractive. That isn't the goal of the Good Shepherd for our lives. In *To Pray and to Grow,* Flora Wuellner affirms:

> This living Jesus Christ not only sees me as I am, in loving forgiveness, but he also releases me from that which makes me unfree. He changes me. In him, we are not only reborn—we grow!
>
> *It is not enough to be made clean through Good Friday. We are to grow in power through Pentecost!*
>
> It was not enough for the prodigal son in Jesus' parable to leave the pigs. The pigs have not yet left him! Safe now in his father's house, he still has bad habits to master and new attitudes to cultivate.
>
> The disciples sitting expectantly in the upper room after Jesus had gone from their sight to the Father, knew they did not yet have what it took to change the world. They knew Jesus loved them,

but they needed to grow in his power to heal the sick, raise the dead, cast out the demonic, and reconcile the hostile.

"Beloved," it was written many years later to the churches, "we are God's children now [security and acceptance]; it does not yet appear what we shall be, but we know that when he appears we shall be like him [expectancy and growth]." (1 John 3:2)

I like what Agnes Sanford said so gloriously. We Christians are to "sit down on the bottom rung of the ladder of sanctity and yell for Jesus Christ."

He will come. He will come as the Good Shepherd to nurture and change us. Don't forget the comparison Jesus made. "The thief comes only to steal and kill and destroy; I came that they may have life and have it abundantly" (John 10:10).

The priorities of the shepherd are to know his own, to nurture his own, and now this third priority—to *protect* his own. Is there a more dramatic word, a more hope-inspiring, a more courage-providing, a more strength-giving word than that of Jesus: "I lay down my life for the sheep"? One of the highest priorities of the Good Shepherd is to protect his own. Think about what that means for us.

What do you fear most in life?

- *Failure?* I was with a forty-two-year-old man recently who is paralyzed in his profession, almost unable to function, because he is afraid he is going to fail.

- *Old age?* More people than you can imagine fear old age, afraid they will lack the necessary financial resources in retirement, wondering if their children will care enough to stand with them and love them through their twilight years.

- *Broken relationships?* Is that your fear? Your marriage is on rocky ground—the spark is not there—the relationship has been treated too casually, even callously. A lot of pain, heartbreak, and damage have accumulated, and you don't know whether the relationship will survive. You're afraid.

- *Your child's future?* Many parents are in the grip of a subtle kind of fear in relation to their children. It's hard to deal with because it is difficult to name, difficult to get a handle on. We are fearful about their lifestyles. There are so many temptations—drugs are so common. We are anxious about the vocation they will choose, the marriage partner they will select. We are fearful that war will come, and they will go.

The list could go on for fear is rampant: the temptation of sexual lust; the tightrope of compromise you've been walking; the competition in business that is pressing so hard, driving you in ways you don't want to go, threatening your integrity.

It is good to name our fear, if we can· face it head-on. Equally important is to know. that the Good Shepherd will protect us from all that we fear. Accept the promise.

You remember the promise of the most beloved shepherd psalm, Psalm 23:

> Even though I walk through the valley of the shadow of death, I fear no evil; for thou art with me. . . . Thou preparest a table before me in the presence of my enemies. . . . Surely goodness and mercy shall follow me all the days of my life; and I shall dwell in the house of the Lord forever.
>
> —Psalm 23:4–6

That's the protection of the Shepherd. He will lay down his life for his sheep.

There are conditions that we must meet, however. The Good Shepherd will protect us only if we allow him. You see, it's one thing for the Shepherd to know us, it's another thing for us to know his voice and follow his instruction. Two things are necessary for us to live under the protection of the Shepherd. First, we have to cultivate hearing and knowing his voice. We do that primarily through prayer, scripture, worship, and sharing with other Christians. To hear the Shepherd's voice we must be within earshot, close enough that we will not miss his call. The commitment of the Shepherd to us, his vigilance in caring for us and guiding us, is to no avail if we wander beyond his protective love. We must be attentive. Everything depends upon our willingness to listen.

Second, we have to practice obedience. When we hear the Shepherd's voice, however it comes, we must obey. The Shepherd disciplines his sheep. We, also, must discipline ourselves in obedience. We begin with little things. We practice responding to the call of Christ in our simple everyday living, so that when the "big" calls come, we will obey.

The secret of living under the protection of the Shepherd is our realization that we do not have to depend upon our own strength, our own willpower, our own good intention, our own self-confidence. We become truly confident when we give up confidence in ourselves and place our confidence in the protection of the Good Shepherd who has promised that he will lay down his life for us.

We've talked about the picture of the Shepherd and the priorities of the Shepherd, now a final, brief word about the *power* of the Shepherd. See it in Jesus' words:

> For this reason, the Father loves me, because I lay down my life, that I may take it again. No one takes it from me, but I lay it down of my own accord. I have power to lay it down, and I have power to take it again; this charge I have received from my Father.

The gospel of the cross is incomplete without this understanding: Christ's death was a death absolutely *self-determined*. He did it by choice. He had power to lay down his life; he had power to keep it. He could have been delivered. Look at him and listen to him in Gethsemane. He could have called for twelve legions of angels to deliver him. Instead, he prayed, "Not as I will, but as thou wilt" (Matt. 26:39). So there is more in this sacrifice of Christ than in the death of a shepherd who dies seeking to protect his sheep. More here than a selfless sacrifice to inspire noble living. Jesus didn't lose his life; he gave it. He was not killed; he chose to die. As all-powerful as Rome was, as firmly in control as the religious establishment of Israel was, those powers did not thrust the cross on Jesus. He took the cross voluntarily—*for us*.

Oh, hear that! Let the truth of it burrow its way into your soul. The Good Shepherd had the power to take up his life or lay it down. He laid it down on the cross—poured out every last drop of blood, sweated in pain until there was no more water of life in him—and he did it for you and me. No wonder the gospel songwriter Stuart Hamblen put it so starkly and so powerfully in "He Bought My Soul":

> Each drop of blood bought me a million years;
> A soul was born each time he shed a tear;
> He loosed the chains that fetter you and me;
> He bought my soul from death at Calvary.

Sometimes a contemporary human experience gives us a picture of the eternal. I read a story awhile ago that was this sort of picture. On a construction site, a man saw that his son was going to be caught in a cave-in. Instantly, he jumped into the hole, hovered over his son, and took the full blow of the collapsing dirt walls. When the workers uncovered them, they found the father dead from a blow on the head, but the son was living. The father's body had kept the dirt off him and enabled him to breathe until the workers saved him.

That is a picture of the Good Shepherd, a hint of what he does for us. His priorities are to know us, to nurture us, to protect us, and, finally, to save us. So he lays down his life on the cross, hovers over us in his death until we breathe the power of his resurrection and life.

We can't ask for more than that, can we? We don't even have to ask for it. The Good Shepherd has already acted in our behalf.

3

I Am the Door

Jesus said, "Truly, truly, I say to you, he who does not enter the sheepfold by the door but climbs in by another way, that man is a thief and a robber; but he who enters by the door is the shepherd of the sheep. To him the gatekeeper opens; the sheep hear his voice, and he calls his own sheep by name and leads them out. When he has brought out all his own, he goes before them, and the sheep follow him, for they know his voice. A stranger they will not follow, but they will flee from him, for they do not know the voice of strangers." This figure Jesus used with them, but they did not understand what he was saying to them.

So Jesus again said to them, "Truly, truly, I say to you, I am the door of the sheep. All who came before me are thieves and robbers; but the sheep did not heed them. I am the door; if any one enters by me, he will be saved, and will go in and out and find pasture. The thief comes only to steal and kill and destroy; I came that they may have life, and have it abundantly."

—John 10:1–10

We never know a person until we know how that person perceives himself. There is no clearer picture of a person than what comes through the self-revelation that person shares with us. Haven't you shared with someone when pretensions were dissolved, defenses fell, honesty prevailed, and you sat on the edge of your seat as the person trusted you by sharing his or her innermost self-understanding and self-appraisal? That's the occasion when persons truly meet; soul touches soul and deep calls to deep. When it is the son of God who does this, the intensity and revelation level is increased a hundredfold.

In this chapter we center on another of those bold claims of Jesus: "I am the door." The image is a vivid one and offers an almost limitless range of possibilities for reflection. The temptation is to put the mind in high gear and pursue all of the openings and nuances suggested by the image of Christ as the door. Instead, let's just plow one furrow deeply. We will do it in words that won't take long to read, but we can take the rest of our lives to cultivate what they mean.

The theme of this chapter is so disarmingly simple. Christ is the door! What is the purpose of a door? *To shut something behind us and to open something to us.* Is that too simple? Don't be victimized by the paralysis of analysis. Symbols themselves are doors, openings for us to reflect upon and experience.

Jesus' claim to be the door is set in the context of the story of the Good Shepherd which we began to consider in the previous chapter. His hearers couldn't understand the meaning, so Jesus plainly, boldly, and without reservation, applied the story to himself, saying, "I am the door of the sheep. . . . if any one enters by me, he will be saved, and will go in and out and find pasture."

In the last chapter we mentioned two kinds of sheepfolds. That image is crucial in Jesus' claim to be the door, so get the picture clearly in mind. There were communal sheepfolds in the villages and towns. All the flocks of the shepherds were sheltered in these large folds at night. A keeper of the fold was hired to protect the sheep and to prevent thievery. Only the keeper had a key to the door, and only a known shepherd was allowed entrance. It was this kind of fold that Jesus was referring to in John 10:1–3, when he talked about robbers climbing in by another way, and the sheep knowing the shepherd's voice.

But there was another kind of fold out in the hills, far from the villages, in the pastures where the shepherds would take their sheep during the warm season. Keeping them there for weeks, the shepherds would build folds in which to keep their sheep at night. These folds were simply open spaces enclosed by a fence. There was no door, only an opening in the fence by which the sheep would go in and out. The shepherd would lie down in that opening at night. No sheep could get in or out except over his body.

It was this kind of sheepfold Jesus was talking about when he said, "I am the door." In the most literal sense, the shepherd was the door; there was no access to the sheepfold except through him.

With that image, the focus of this chapter is disarmingly simple. *The purpose of a door is to shut something behind us and to open something to us.*

Christ is the door: "If any one enters by me, he will be saved." What does it mean to be saved and to enter the sheepfold of the Good Shepherd and shut something behind us?

At the very heart of it, it means that through Christ we shut the door to an old life of sin and guilt, pain and loss. Now doesn't that sound fundamental? It is, but I don't know anything more desperately needed by persons today than to know that their sins are forgiven, that their guilt can be taken away—to know that the door has been closed on the past and that they are accepted by God. The New Testament abounds with promises which too many of us have not yet appropriated. "The saying is sure and worthy of full acceptance, that Christ Jesus came into the world to save sinners" (1 Tim. 1:15). "It is not the healthy that need a doctor, but the sick; I have not come to invite virtuous people, but to call sinners to repentance" (Luke 5:31, NEB). "God shows his love for us in that while we were yet sinners Christ died for us" (Rom. 5:8).

Acknowledging oneself a sinner and becoming personally aware of God's forgiveness is the central event that makes a person a Christian. Does that sound awfully old-fashioned? It is the heartbeat of the gospel and the core of the Christian experience. Live with the idea for a moment. Do you remember Psalm 51?

> Have mercy on me, O God,
>   according to thy steadfast love;

according to thy abundant mercy
blot out my transgressions.
Wash me thoroughly from my iniquity,
and cleanse me from my sin!
For I know my transgressions,
and my sin is ever before me.
—Psalm 51:1–3

Create in me a clean heart, O God,
and put a new and right spirit within
me.
Cast me not away from thy presence,
and take not thy holy Spirit from me.
Restore to me the joy of thy salvation.
—Psalm 51:10–12

Do you feel the throbbing intensity of that prayer? There is nothing perfunctory about it. It is no surface recitation of some pious words labeled "prayer." These are not pet phrases packaged mechanically together and tied with the dainty ribbon, "In Jesus' name. Amen." This is true prayer, the heart-cry of a broken man.

Ancient editors say that Psalm 51 is David's anguished cry for forgiveness and cleansing after he had faced up to his blatant sin with Bathsheba. The prophet Nathan confronted David with his lust, adultery, intrigue, pretense, and sham. He reminded David of how he had schemed to get his trusted servant Uriah murdered. The king of Israel had deliberately broken five of the Ten Commandments.

David had no escape; the secret was out. Yet as we read the psalm, we feel that there was a kind of relief. The hidden thing had surfaced. The cancer that was eating David's soul away was now exposed and labeled for what it was. The need for subterfuge and deception was over.

Have you ever experienced the relief that comes when you no longer have to hide, when the truth is known and you no longer have to live a lie? That's the meaning of confession: the end of pretension, coming out of hiding.

I remember a vivid illustration of this. A dynamic, young Christian couple had the world and the future in their hands. However, they did not carefully consider their sexual relationship, and she became pregnant before their marriage. Without counseling with anyone, they decided on abortion. They married, and life seemed to go well for a while; both were successful in their work. Then they decided to have children. When I met them, she had been pregnant twice, but had miscarried both times. Pregnant again, she was devastated by anxiety.

In a rush of tears she poured out her feelings of guilt over the premarital sexual relationship and the abortion. She believed that her miscarriages were God's punishment for her earlier decisions—decisions she now felt had been mistakes. I assured her that God's love for her had never faltered. The couple made a new commitment to Christ, and allowed him to shut the door on their past pain. They were once again able to face the future with joy and assurance.

Most of our needs are not that dramatic. But rare is the person who doesn't need Christ to shut the door on some painful past experience. You know the pain, and don't need to be reminded of it. But maybe you do need to be reminded of the promise of the psalmist: "As far as the east is from the west, so far does he remove our transgressions from us" (Psalm 103:12).

We need Christ to help us shut the door on many painful experiences. Have you allowed Christ to be the shut door of that painful experience that tore your family apart? What about the untimely death of a loved one? You feel cheated. The loss is still painful, the emptiness still gnaws at your gut, and you find yourself questioning God. Bitterness puts knots in your stomach and makes life taste sour.

There is another kind of pain for which there needs to be healing, against which Christ would like to shut the door. It's the pain of what I call "lost time." It may be time lost by an alcoholic or time lost by a father from his family, because he put his profession first. Perhaps things are changed now. The alcoholic is healed, the father has a whole new perspective. But damage has been done, and pain is still there. Christ wants to heal you and close the door on that past!

With Jesus' claim is our promise: Christ is the door, the door that can close behind us all our past sin and guilt, all the pain and anguish we have experienced. It is only as we accept this fact that we can move to what Christ as *the door* opens to us. That is our next consideration.

Not only are persons saved, delivered, and healed through Christ, who is the door, closing something behind us; if we enter through Christ, the door, the next phrase of scripture says we will "go in and out and find pasture."

It is a beautiful image of being *protected* and

sustained. Jesus follows it up with a word that makes it even clearer. "I came that they may have life, and have it abundantly." So, Jesus is the door to something and that something is life, life of a quality that can be ours only through Christ.

What is the essence of this life that is ours through Christ? It is a life of trustful relationship with God and loving service to our neighbors. First, let's look at a life of trustful relationship with God. One illustration will make it clear.

In an article in *alive now!* (May/June 1980), Ted Schroeder tells about when he was a young preacher in his first appointment, and the challenges and problems of that parish raised many doubts. Then he met Grandma Sudley. He would visit Grandma Sudley when he wanted to say he was making shut-in calls but did not want to listen to any more painful stories. When he just wanted to visit a friend, he would go to see Grandma Sudley.

> "How are the old ladies?" she would say.
> "They're still after me," I would say.
> "Not me," she would say.
> "Not me. I've had enough of getting breakfast for some lazy man. . . ."
> She would ask me to say a prayer with her just so I would feel like I was doing my job, even though both of us knew she prayed oftener and better than I ever thought of.
> Now she was dying.

The young minister felt totally inadequate as he entered the hospital. The family had all gathered and they looked to him, assuming he knew what to do. He didn't. The nurse told him he could go in to see Grandma. He hesitated, and finally went into the room.

Grandma looked so tired. She was breathing hard. They had a tube in her nose and some other tubes in her arms. They were dripping.

"God help me." It was the best prayer I could think of. I stood there for a while hoping that she would not wake up. Then she opened her eyes and saw me. She smiled.

"How are all your old ladies?" she said in a whisper.

"Still trying to get me." I tried to smile, too.

"Not me," she said.

There was silence for a long time. I held her hand. It was hard and soft and brittle. After a while she looked at me again.

"I guess I'm going to leave," she said.

"I know," I said.

"I'm very tired."

"I know," I said again.

"I've never died before," she smiled again a little bit.

"I've never been with someone who died before," I said.

"I think we'll make it, Pastor." She was almost whispering. She squeezed my hand a little.

"Will you listen while I pray?" Her eyes were closed. I did not answer. She knew what I would say.

"My Father," she whispered, "take me home because of my Jesus. And Father, take care of this good boy here. He has given love, and he has been my friend. Amen."

I was crying. "Thank you, Grandma," I said.

"It's all right. I'm just going to be with a friend. Tell them out there that I'm all right."

"I'll tell them, Grandma," I said.

Grandma Sudley found it, and the young minister, now a leading clergyman, learned it from her: Christ is the door to a life of trustful relationship with God, a relationship which sees us not only through life but through death.

Now the other part of this truth. The life Jesus opens to us is one of *loving service to our neighbor*. Through him we "go in and out and find pasture." That going out is as important as the coming in. The Good Shepherd was willing to lay down his life for his sheep. If he is our door to life, nothing is more characteristic of the life he offers us than loving service to our neighbor.

Washington Gladden was a preacher nearly as famous at the turn of the century as Billy Graham is now. He tells in his *Recollections* of the agonies he experienced because he felt he could not find Christ. He had been taught, and he thoroughly believed, that he needed to make his peace with God, accept Christ and be born again. He tried for years to gain the assurance of divine love. He listened intently in prayer meetings to the testimony of those who had found it; he attended every revival meeting which came along; he followed the suggestions which others prescribed. He tried to surrender himself a thousand times, but nothing seemed to happen. He never seemed to find or feel what others did. Many nights, from his little unplastered room under the rafters of his father's farmhouse, he looked out at the stars with perplexity of spirit because he had not found Christ.

Then one day he met a minister who was sensitive, caring, and clear-headed. He told Gladden that if he would do his best to walk in the ways of loving service, he could trust God's love whether he had any raptures or ecstatic experiences about it or not. That was the word he needed. Washington Gladden began to walk where Jesus walked. He was led into a life of notable ministry. He brought incisive application of the gospel to the social issues of the day, and helped shape the history of the church in America. It is little wonder that he could write:

> O Master, let me walk with thee
> In lowly paths of service free;
> Tell me thy secret; help me bear
> The strain of toil, the fret of care.
>
> Help me the slow of heart to move
> By some clear, winning word of love;
> Teach me the wayward feet to stay,
> And guide them in the home-ward way.

He had found the life of loving service to our neighbor which Christ opens to us.

"I am the door," said Jesus, "if any one enters by me, he will be saved, and will go in and out and find pasture." Jesus is saying to us, "I will shut the past of sin and guilt and pain and loss out; I will open the door to an abundant life—a life of trustful dependence upon God, and loving service to your neighbor" (AP).

In Jesus' claim is our promise, so we must remember: the important thing about doors is that they mean nothing unless we use them.

4

I Am the True Vine

I am the true vine, and my Father is the vine-dresser. Every branch of mine that bears no fruit, he takes away, and every branch that does bear fruit he prunes, that it may bear more fruit. You are already made clean by the word which I have spoken to you. Abide in me, and I in you. As the branch cannot bear fruit by itself, unless it abides in the vine, neither can you, unless you abide in me. I am the vine, you are the branches. He who abides in me, and I in him, he it is that bears much fruit, for apart from me you can do nothing. If a man does not abide in me, he is cast forth as a branch and withers; and the branches are gathered, thrown into the fire and burned. If you abide in me, and my words abide in you, ask whatever you will, and it shall be done for you. By this my Father is glorified, that you bear much fruit, and so prove to be my disciples. As the Father has loved me, so have I loved you; abide in my love. If you keep my commandments, you will abide in my love, just as I have kept my Father's commandments and abide in his love. These things I have spoken to you, that my joy may be in you, and that your joy may be full.

John 15:1–11

Jesus was the master of figurative language. He used parables to communicate his great truths. He told stories, painted word pictures, or called attention to ordinary things to express extraordinary and eternal truths.

In John's Gospel, there is more of the figurative speech, the metaphor, than the short story, the parables that we have in the other Gospels. Many of Jesus' great claims are familiar images with which the listener is able to immediately identify. This is certainly true of the claim we consider in this chapter: "I am the true vine."

Jesus' disciples would certainly have identified with the symbol of the vine and the branches, pruning and fruit-bearing, dead branches burned. They could identify with it because Palestine was a vineyard country, and grapes were a common fruit of the land. But more than that, these disciples, Jews that they were, knew the vine as the symbol for Israel. Over and over again in the Old Testament, Israel is pictured as the vine or the vineyard of God.

In Isaiah 5:1-7, the prophet Isaiah pictures Israel as the vineyard of God. "The vineyard of the Lord of hosts is the house of Israel" (Isa. 5:7). Jeremiah quotes God's word to Israel: "I planted you a choice vine" (Jer. 2:21). And Hosea puts it as a word of judgment: "Israel is an empty vine" (Hos. 10:1, KJV). Thinking of God's deliverance of his people from bondage, the psalmist sang, "Thou didst bring a vine out of Egypt" (Psalm 80:8).

It takes only a little imagination to put Jesus' word in the setting that would register an overwhelming impact on the disciples. According to

John's word in chapter 13, Jesus had finished the Passover meal with his disciples, having confronted the disciples, Judas in particular, with his betrayal and impending death. In Matthew 26 we learn that they walked from the place of the Last Supper to the Garden of Gethsemane. Jesus talked to the disciples as they went to this place where Jesus would make his final surrender: "Not as I will, but as thou wilt" (Matt. 26:39).

They must have passed near the Temple. Over the doors of that great place, exquisitely carved and covered with goldleaf, was the grapevine, the symbol of Israel. Josephus is reported to have said that the golden vine and clusters were as large as a man. With what pride must the disciples have looked upon that. They were a part of Israel, the vine whose roots stem from Abraham, Isaac, and Jacob. They were a part of the chosen race. In spite of Rome, God would protect the vine, and he would send a Messiah who would deliver them.

The disciples had been with Jesus nearly three years now, but it was still confusing. They were still not sure what it was all about, nor were they unshakably sure as to why they were following him.

We are not a part of that chosen people—the divine community, the vine—as were the disciples, so we have to live with Jesus' word, "I am the true vine," for it to have any meaning. How shocking this word of Jesus must have been to the disciples. In one unveiled, unreserved, undiluted claim, Jesus shattered the smug complacency of Israel. He pierced the proud exclusiveness of the Jews. They were more than the vine, they were God's vineyard.

"I am the true vine," was Jesus' shattering word, "and anyone who loves me—not just the descendants of Abraham, Isaac, and Jacob, not just those who have been circumcised, but *anyone* who loves me—they are the branches" (AP). Those disciples got the message. Let's try to get it. In this chapter we will lift three words out of the scripture passage as pegs upon which we can hang our thoughts, simple words that capture the essence of this great claim of Jesus. The words are *abide, apart,* and *ask.*

The first is the key word *abide.* It occurs ten times in the first eleven verses of John 15. It is a crucial word in Jesus' faith vocabulary. So, let's seek to probe its meaning and apply it to our lives. The noun expression of the Greek word is *monē,* the word Jesus used in John 14:2 when he said, "In my Father's house are many rooms," or many dwelling places. Jesus is assuring his disciples and all who will ever trust him that the goal of our lives, the end toward which it all moves, is to dwell in the presence of God forever. As a verb, this Greek noun for dwelling place means "remain" or "abide."

Get the connection now. It is a part of Jesus' last instruction to his disciples before his death. In the thirteenth and fourteenth chapters of John, he talked about his death. This deeply disturbed and confused the disciples. So Jesus was saying to them, "Don't be confused, don't be troubled, don't give way to despair even though I will soon leave you. Believe in my love and trustworthiness, put your weight of faith upon me, and you will find a safe abiding place. I promise it. Even though I go, I will return and receive you unto myself, that where I am you may be also" (AP).

The word *abide* has even more power than *dwelling place*. It has to do with relationship, not physical location. And the astounding truth is this: You and I can dwell in the Father, and the Father and the Son will dwell in us by the Holy Spirit. That can happen as we *abide* in Christ.

Let's be even more specific. What does it mean to abide in Christ? It means at least three things: realizing his presence, responding to his prodding and probing, and resting in his peace.

To realize is to make real. So how do we realize Christ's presence? In three primary ways: prayer, scripture, and worship.

"Abide in me," Jesus said. That certainly has a mystical meaning to it, yet we do not have to be mystics to pray and experience the presence of Christ. Thomas Aquinas once reportedly said to Bonaventura, "Show me your library." Bonaventura took Thomas Aquinas to his cell and pointed to a crucifix before which he prayed. "There it is," he said.

That is the heart of the Christian life, certainly the heart of prayer—waiting upon the Lord, especially waiting before the crucified Lord in order to stay aware of his sacrificial love for us, the cost of our salvation. "But," you say, "I pray, and I don't feel anything; I don't sense Christ's presence. Nothing seems to be happening." I understand. You are not alone. It happens to us all. That's the reason we begin at this point: we must *realize,* make real, Christ's presence.

That is also the reason scripture is so important. I'm certain of it. The prayer life of most of us is dry and barren because we do not live with the scripture. I ask you now, do you have a quiet time with the Lord each day? A time when you live with a portion of scripture, let that scripture speak to you, then speak to God out of God having spoken to you through his word? The Bible is not to adorn our coffee tables, but to adorn our lives. It is not for show; it is for our salvation.

Then there is worship. We need not only our private worship in our daily quiet time, but corporate worship in which we come together with the community of faith to praise God, to rehearse and celebrate God's saving acts in history, to confess and receive pardon, to hear God's word preached, and receive that word as our marching orders.

Frederick B. Speakman has suggested that the man who has nothing before which he is eager to bow will some day be flattened by the sheer weight of himself. One of our biggest problems is that we have lost the sense of the holy. That before which we are eager to bow is not sacred, but secular and profane. We bow before our jobs and the success of our professions. We humble ourselves before the crass materialism in the world around us that is squeezing us into its mold. We're driven by our passions and the lusts of our flesh. Security is more central in our minds than our salvation. We've lost, if we ever had, the "fear of God." We don't tremble in God's presence; in fact, we evade rather than seek God's presence.

If we're going to abide in Christ, we must realize his presence, and we do that through prayer, scripture, and worship.

We abide in Christ by realizing his presence, and we also abide in Christ by responding to his prodding and probing. Be sure of this. He does probe. He does prod. This prodding and probing comes to us in our quiet time, when we pray and live with the scripture, when we allow the written word of God to become the living word in our souls every day. It also comes through the preached word.

Through preaching, Christ probes and prods. Sometimes he afflicts us in our comfort, and sometimes he comforts us in our affliction. If we are to abide in Christ, we must respond to that prodding and probing.

Christ also prods and probes through our friends, through other people, people who care enough about us to be honest, to speak the truth in love. I don't know of a more effective way of abiding in Christ than by making a covenant with friends to pray for each other, to hold each other accountable, and to speak the truth to each other in love. Imagine how Christ would prod and probe if you agreed with your wife or husband or with two or three friends to take a special time each week, maybe thirty minutes, to ask each other questions like this:

At what moment this past week did you feel closest to Christ?

At what moment during this week did you feel you were responding to God's call to be a disciple?

When was your faith tested this week through failure or by a great demand being made of you?

Christ prods and probes us not only through our friends and loved ones and special times of sharing, but also through the witness of other people whom we simply observe and listen to—maybe even strangers, as I noted in this account of John Wesley in *The Sanctuary for Lent 1984.*

During Wesley's student days, a poor porter knocked on Wesley's door one evening and asked to speak with him. During the conversation, Wesley observed the man's thin coat. It was a cold night, and Wesley suggested that he had better get another coat. "This is the only coat I have," the porter replied, "and I thank God for it."

Wesley asked the man if he had eaten and the porter answered, "I have had nothing today but water to drink, but I thank God for that."

Wesley, growing uneasy in the man's presence, reminded him that he would have to get to his quarters soon or be locked out. "Then what would you thank God for?" Wesley asked.

"I will thank him," replied the porter, "that I have dry stones to lie upon."

Wesley was deeply moved by the man's sincerity and he said to him, "You thank God when you have nothing to wear, nothing to eat, and no bed to lie on. What else do you thank God for?"

The simple man replied, "I thank God that he has given me life, a heart to love him, and a desire to serve him."

After the man had left with a coat from Wesley's closet, some money for food, and words of appreciation for the witness he had made, Wesley wrote something like this in his journal, "I shall never forget that porter. He convinced me *there is something in religion to which I am a stranger.*"

Pay attention to others. Through them, Christ will prod and probe, and we abide in Christ by responding to his prodding and probing.

How do we abide in Christ? First, by realizing his presence; second, by responding to his prodding and probing; and now third, by *resting in his peace.*

I mean by that not an escape from the world, but a resting in Christ which equips us to be in the world. I mean the sort of thing that can come to us in the midst of noise and din, in the dark night of confusion and suffering, in the tension of temptation and the rigorous demands of the struggle to be morally responsible. The anonymous poet knew the secret of that "resting in his peace."

> There is a viewless, cloistered room,
> As high as heaven, as fair as day,
> Where, though my feet may join the throng,
> My soul can enter in, and pray.
>
> One hearkening, even, cannot know
> When I have crossed the threshold o'er:
> For He alone, who hears my prayer,
> Has heard the shutting of the door.

When we have that, nothing can come that we can't overcome. You have seen it as I have. One person responds to a set of experiences as confusing mysteries, baffling problems, or heavy burdens. Yet the same sort of experiences can be to another the kind of burden that in Samuel Rutherford's phrase, "sails are to a ship, that wings are to a bird."

To one person, life's experiences become dark valleys and steep mountains with rough places in between. Yet to another, every valley is exalted, mountains and hills are brought low, rough places are made plain because that person has found the peace and power of abiding in Christ.

So that's the first word: *abide*. Now the second: *apart*. Apart is a painful word. It's harsh. There's a kind of finality about it. In John 15:5, Jesus says, "Apart from me you can do nothing." That's a prodding and probing word, a challenge. But the painful picture is the judgment that comes if we live our lives apart from Christ. We will be cast forth as a branch that withers; we will be gathered and thrown into the fire and burned.

Isn't that a frightening thought? It is my conviction that we don't think about it enough. Judgment is written into the fabric of life, and the Bible makes clear that one day there will be a final judgment, and each one of us will have to give an account before God.

Don't tell me that God is too loving to condemn any person to eternal hell. That misses the point. God doesn't condemn us to hell; we condemn ourselves. Jesus Christ is loving friend and companion. He is Savior, who wants to be Lord. He does everything, goes even to the limits of the cross, to graft each one of us to the vine, that we might be sustained and saved.

It is those who refuse him, who deny or simply ignore, and by default fail to receive his love and life who are condemned by their own deliberate refusal or failure to act. Do you remember that clear word in Hebrews 4:13 "No creature is hidden, but all are open and laid bare to the eyes of him with whom we have to do"? And Jesus is the one "with whom we have to do."

Also, don't evade the issue by arguing about the nature of hell and eternal separation from Christ. Be assured of this—you will meet Christ one day in an ultimate time of reckoning, when an account will have to be made. The meeting will be a matter of judgment or grace, and what we have been and done will determine which it is.

The cockney soldier in "Well?" by G. A. Studdert Kennedy expressed it very effectively:

> There ain't no throne, and there ain't no books,
> It's 'Im you've got to see,
> It's 'Im, just 'Im, that is the Judge
> Of blokes like you and me.
>
> And, boys, I'd sooner frizzle up
> I' the flames of a burning 'Ell,
> Than stand and look into 'Is face
> And 'ear 'Is voice say, "Well?"

When that dread moment comes and we stand before the judgment bar of God, when we look into Jesus' face, I want to be abiding in Christ, not *apart* from the life-giving vine.

Abide, apart, and now the final word: *ask.* "If you abide in me, and my words abide in you, ask whatever you will, and it shall be done for you" (John 15:7).

An entire chapter could be written on this word alone. It is one of those stupendous promises of Jesus that even when we muster the faith to believe it, we remain baffled, and we don't lay hold of the promise often enough. Let the word about prayer stand as it is.

Focus on this one truth: If we abide in Christ all the rewards of dwelling in him are ours. Answered prayer? Yes! Guidance for our daily living? Yes! Certainty in the midst of confusion? Yes! Strength to be more than conquerors of him who loves us? Yes!

"If you abide in me, and my words abide in you, ask." It is a clear word about relationship. Sometimes we can get a glimpse of the depth of that relationship with Christ in a human relationship.

Marian Anderson and her mother had such a relationship. The beauty of Miss Anderson's music brings one to tears. The beauty of her character brings one to his knees. This is the reason Fannie Hurst was prompted to say, "Marian Anderson has not grown simply great; she has grown great simply." An incident from her life shows the depth and purity of her character and the beauty of her relationship with her mother. Sol Hurok, the concert impresario, once told Billy Rose that he was present when reporters were interviewing the great contralto. They asked her to name the greatest moment in her life. Hurok knew, relates Billy Rose, that she had many to choose from.

There was the night when Toscanini told her that hers was the finest voice of the century. There was the private concert she gave at the White House for the Roosevelts and the king and queen of England. She received the $10,000 Bok Award as the person who had done most for her hometown, Philadelphia. To top it all, there was the Easter Sunday in Washington when she stood beneath the

Lincoln statue and sang for a crowd of 75,000, which included Cabinet members, Supreme Court Justices, and most members of Congress.

"Which of these moments did Marian choose?" Billy Rose asked.

None of them, said the impresario. "Miss Anderson told the reporter that the greatest moment of her life was the day she went home and told her mother she wouldn't have to take in washing any more."

If this magnificent relationship can exist between mother and daughter, how much more magnificent our relationship with Christ can be! "I am the true vine," said Jesus. "As the Father has loved me, so have I loved you; abide in my love." And what will happen? Jesus tells us: "My joy may be in you and . . . your joy may be full."

5

You Say That I Am a King

They led Jesus from the house of Caiaphas to the praetorium. It was early. They themselves did not enter the praetorium, so that they might not be defiled, but might eat the passover. So Pilate went out to them and said, "What accusation do you bring against this man?" They answered him, "If this man were not an evildoer, we would not have handed him over." Pilate said to them, "Take him yourselves and judge him by your own law." The Jews said to him, "It is not lawful for us to put any man to death." This was to fulfil the word which Jesus had spoken to show by what death he was to die.

Pilate entered the praetorium again and called Jesus, and said to him, "Are you the King of the Jews?" Jesus answered, "Do you say this of your own accord, or did others say it to you about me?" Pilate answered, "Am I a Jew? Your own nation and the chief priests have handed you over to me; what have you done?" Jesus answered, "My kingship is not of this world; if my kingship were of this world, my servants would fight, that I might not be handed over to the Jews; but my kingship is not from the world." Pilate said to him, "So you are a king?" Jesus answered, "You say that I am a king. For this I was born, and for this I have come into the world, to bear witness to the truth. Every one who is of the truth hears my voice." Pilate said to him, "What is truth?"

After he had said this, he went out to the Jews again, and told them, "I find no crime in him. But you have a custom that I should release one man for you at the Passover; will you have me release for you the King of the Jews?" They cried out again, "Not this man, but Barabbas!" Now Barabbas was a robber.

—John 18:28–40

It's something for a commoner from rural Mississippi to be in the presence of royalty. I want you to know I even shook the hand of Prince Philip. It was the occasion of the reopening of Wesley's Chapel, London, 1980. It was a great celebration. Methodists from all over the world were there. For the first time in history, a ruling monarch visited a Methodist meeting house. Queen Elizabeth and Prince Philip were there; the prince read one of the scripture lessons.

Later, about 150 of us were invited to a reception for the queen and prince. My wife Jerry and I were there, as excited as all the rest.

I never will forget it, the elegance of it all, but there was something else—an indescribable feeling of anticipation and excitement as we awaited the queen's arrival. I confess I was impressed, inexplainably impressed with the mystique that surrounds royalty.

The sense of excitement and the anticipation grew, and we became almost breathless. Dr. Albert Outler, the eminent Wesley scholar, summed it all up as he said, "For those who have been the ardent champions of democratic institutions for 200 years, now in the presence of royalty, we are quite beside ourselves." And we were! There's something about royalty.

Now, it was no royal scene when Jesus entered Jerusalem on Palm Sunday. Yet, people were quite beside themselves. They were beside themselves because "King Jesus," a king unlike any other, was turning their world upside down. It was a paradoxical scene that Palm Sunday 2,000 years ago. Harry Kemp reflected upon it in his poem, "The Conquerors":

> I saw the Conquerors riding by
>   With cruel lips and faces wan:
> Musing on kingdoms sacked and burned
>   There rode the Mongol Genghis Khan;
>
> And Alexander, like a god,
>   Who sought to weld the world in one:
> And Caesar with his laurel wreath;
>   And like a thing from Hell, the Hun:
>
> And leading like a star the van,
>   Heedless of upstretched arm and groan,
> Inscrutable Napoleon went
>   Dreaming of empire, and alone . . .
>
> Then all they perished from the earth.
>   As fleeting shadows from a glass,
> And, conquering down the centuries,
>   Came Christ, the Swordless, on an ass!

The people who greet Jesus on the day of his entry are unaware of the intrigue among the powerful in Jerusalem. Each Gospel tells the story of their entry. The crowds wave palm branches and shout, "Hosanna!" This is highly symbolic. Palm branches were a sign of praise and celebration. They were used for the procession during the Feast of Tabernacles and were also used by Judas Maccabeus in the ceremony of the Rededication of the Temple more than a hundred years later.

"Blessed is he who comes in the name of the Lord, even the King of Israel!" (John 12:13) was the shout of the people, according to all the Gospels. This is a shout of praise, but also a cry for help. It is from Psalm 118 which was used in the celebration of the Feasts of Tabernacles, Dedication, and Passover. The word *Hosanna* means "Help us please."

Here is a study in contrasts. Jesus entered Jerusalem on a lowly donkey—no pomp and circumstance for him, no staging of a media event. Undoubtedly that very week, since it was Passover, the people had witnessed the dramatic and gala entry into their city of Herod and his entourage. Pilate also would have come in great splendor. Both these government leaders lived away from Jerusalem, but at times of great feasts, they would make an appearance. Such occasions were good times for the show of Roman power, and a Roman parade would communicate that—a great golden Roman eagle leading the way, followed by pennants of Rome, then soldiers and chariots.

In contrast to all that—Jesus on a donkey. Yet the crowds respond differently. They sense who Jesus is. There is a shock of recognition, and they greet him with adulation, "Hosanna! Blessed is he who comes in the name of the Lord." That changed, of course. A few days later the "Hosannas" had become screams of hatred and derision: "Crucify him!"

He had been arrested and brought before Pilate, and there we hear the claim which we consider in this chapter. This claim is different from the others we have looked at. In fact it is not an outright claim; it is a response to the controversy that swirled around the accusation that he claimed to be a king. Luke records in his Gospel that "the whole company of them arose, and brought him before Pilate. And they began to accuse him, saying, 'We found this man perverting our nation, and forbidding us to give tribute to Caesar, and saying that he himself is Christ a king'" (Luke 23:1–2).

Pilate must have been terribly confused when this lonely one stood before him, hands bound behind, face pale with sorrow and mental anguish. *What is this,* Pilate sneers beneath his breath. *What are these crazy, strange Jews up to now?* Then he sneers aloud: "You? Are you a king?"

What a dilemma Jesus faced! Note with wonder his response. A yes or a no would have left a false impression. A yes would be a guilty plea in Pilate's mind. A no would have been a denial of a deeper truth, for in the most real sense he was, is, and will be forever a king. So Jesus said: "You say that I am a king. For this I was born, and for this I have come into the world." In Pilate's sense of the word *king,* the answer was "No!" In the deepest sense of the word, the answer was "Yes!" It is in this deeper sense that this claim of Jesus demands our rapt attention as we seek to discover in his claim our promise.

Before we deal specifically with the meaning

of this claim of Jesus, let's take a sweeping look at the scripture setting from which it comes and garner some relevant truths for our lives. There are three major lessons which I label in this fashion: the deadly poison of hatred, the degenerate prostitution of power, the distorted perception of religion.

First, let us consider the deadly poison of hatred. Hatred is a terrible thing. Nothing in the world distorts reality as hatred does. It drives us to twist the truth and act irrationally. It is a kind of madness. Once we allow ourselves to hate, we lose control of ourselves. We can neither see clearly nor act responsibly.

That's what happened to the Jews. They began by hating Jesus because he was a threat to their religious system, to everything they held holy. Their hatred became hysteria. It turned them into a maddened, shrieking crowd who called for Jesus' death.

But move from that scene 2,000 years ago to the present. Hatred still perverts and poisons us. I never will forget those tumultuous days of racial upheaval in Mississippi in the late 1950s and early 1960s. It was not restricted to Mississippi; it was all over the nation, but I was a pastor in Mississippi, so that's what I knew firsthand. I can still see the twisted faces, flushed with blood rushing to their heads; I can still hear the venomous anger spewing from otherwise calm, upright, educated, religious folks at a meeting called to discuss the public stand I had taken for public schools, freedom of the pulpit, and voter rights.

I never will forget the mob that surrounded a

black church in Gulfport, Mississippi, when a meeting ended at which a white missionary from South Africa had spoken against the sinful, oppressive system of apartheid in that nation. A few of us whites were there and the establishment thought there was something clandestine and subversive about it. I never will forget the fear in the voice of the pastor of that black Methodist church when he called me at midnight. The police chief was in his home demanding that the pastor give him the name of every white person at that meeting.

Hatred perverts our thinking, poisons our emotions, and causes us to act in ways that we would flee from under normal circumstances. And it is not always dramatic.

I've seen people go for years estranged from members of their family because of hatred. I've seen people dry up inside, turn into hard, calloused, uncaring people because somewhere along the way someone did something bad to them, hurt them. Rather than dealing with it redemptively, they chose to hate. I've even known married people who simply marked time in their relationship, acted civilly most of the time, but who were eaten up by hatred for their spouses.

Learn this lesson well. The deadly poison of hatred will pervert and destroy you. No wonder Paul said, "Do not let the sun go down on your anger" (Eph. 4:26). He knew the destructive poison that harbored hatred releases in the person. In addition to the deadly perversion of hatred, there is a second lesson here: the degenerate prostitution of power. You see it in scripture, particularly in two people. Caiaphas, the high priest, fell into the snare that tempts us all at one time or another, the snare of the end justifying the means. It was, according to Caiaphas, "expedient that one man should die for the people" (John 18:14).

And look at Pilate. In *The Intimate Gospel: Studies in John,* Earl F. Palmer describes Pilate's awesome decision.

> When the moment of decision confronts him it is obvious that the way of justice requires time, time for Pilate as a judge to weigh and think, but that to take that time requires tremendous inner strength and courage in the face of a potential riot. Pilate does not have that courage, and therefore, at the greatest crossroad moment of his life, he makes an awesome decision based upon the show of immediate power and the preservation of self-interest.
>
> The dialogue between Jesus and this Roman official has placed squarely onto the stage of human history the great tension present at the moment of all important moral decisions. It is the tension between truth and power. Of the two, power has all of the immediate advantages. It is the power of the crowd that takes away from Pilate the necessary time to think. It is the power of Pilate that makes him think he is able to set aside the question of truth. The decisive moment only takes a few seconds' time, but the consequences will last throughout all time.

I saw a cartoon recently of two persons talking about the political situation. "What do you think of the two candidates?" one asked. The other responded, "I'm glad we can elect only one of them to office." That suggests our cynicism about politics and power. We know it firsthand in our state and in our nation. The degenerate prostitution of power. We saw it in the criminal activity surrounding Governor Blanton of Tennessee, and the paroling of prisoners for monetary gain. We saw it in the frightening white light of Watergate.

An article in *The New Yorker* (Sept. 12, 1983) reflected upon the gathering at the Lincoln Memorial last year to commemorate the twentieth anniversary of the march on Washington and Martin Luther King's "I Have a Dream" speech. The author of that article said about that gathering:

> What we ourself were struck by was that the strategies people propose for putting an end to the remaining tragedies differed subtly but decisively from the King approach. Instead of looking to individual hearts for change, the men and women who stood before the microphones last month in Washington were looking to the legislatures, to the polling places. Altering the political landscape, not the moral anatomy, concerned them; in speech after speech, the stress was on trouncing Reagan, on registering voters in awesome numbers.

Then he stated the difference between the present strategy and that of King:

> Deeply convinced that somewhere inside all men there lives an abiding notion of right and wrong, King and his followers used suffering and courage to bring that notion of shame and dignity to the surface. "Unearned suffering is redemptive," he told the crowd by the reflecting pool twenty years ago, and in an almost miraculous way he was correct. He and his methods redeemed lives—not only the lives of black men and women, who found a new sense of worth, but also the lives of white men and women, who found, at the least, a new

sense of guilt and, at the best, an ideal concern and love.

Whatever you think of Martin Luther King, he put power in proper perspective, and the whole world is indebted to him for bringing into focus the truth that can never be denied. James Russell Lowell put it this way:

> Though the cause of evil prosper,
> Yet 'tis truth alone is strong;
> Though her portion be the scaffold,
> And upon the throne be wrong:
> Yet that scaffold sways the future,
> And, behind the dim unknown,
> Standeth God within the shadow
> Keeping watch above his own.

Go back to Caiaphas now. He said that it was "expedient that one man should die for the people" (John 18:14). His was a degenerate prostitution of power. But to show how God prevails, what Caiaphas said in that prostituted notion of power became true. Jesus did die for the people, but it was not a matter of expediency. It was a matter of the eternal will of God and shows forever the nature of the prevailing power of sacrificial love.

Not only the deadly poison of hatred and the degenerate prostitution of power, but there is a third truth here: the distorted perception of religion. The people who were condemning Jesus were religious; they were religious beyond reason. The deadly fact is that their religion distorted their perception of life, rightness, truth, and ultimate value.

Jesus' accusers, Jewish religious leaders, brought him from Caiaphas' house to Pilate in the praetorium. They would not enter the praetorium for fear of defilement, which would make them unfit for the Passover meal. What does all this mean? The law of the Jews was very strict, often rigid beyond reason. The law said the houses of Gentiles were defiled and no Jew should enter. If Jews entered, they must then purify themselves by ceremonial cleansing.

So the picture comes clear. They were abiding by the law with absolute, meticulous care; at the same time they were hounding to the cross the noble son of God.

It is easy to turn our religion into a set of rules and regulations, easy to keep the letter of the law and completely miss the point and the spirit. A recent movie, *Footloose,* is an illustration. Many people seeing the movie may not get beyond the fantastic choreography, music, dancing, and the dominant conflict between teenage culture and unfeeling, uncaring adults. The deeper message of the film is that a preacher, reacting to the pain and loss of a son who died in an auto accident caused by drunkenness, turned an entire town into a company of Pharisees with a distorted perception of religion. He lost his family in the process and had to deal with the fallout of mad people burning library books, oppressing people, and becoming personal, moral policemen for everyone else.

It is easy at every level of life to confess religious principles and crucify love. It is easy to be religious but not live righteously. Righteousness requires giving cups of cold water in Jesus' name; it means doing it unto "the least of these" as we would do it unto Christ—visiting the sick, feeding the hungry, ministering to prisoners, living out the "acceptable year of the Lord." It means risking defilement by going into the houses of Pilate, risking identification with the shadowy side of life.

William Temple, Archbishop of Canterbury, put it clearly: The church is "the only cooperative society in the world that exists for the benefit of its non-members." He was only echoing what Jesus said, "Those who are well have no need of a physician, but those who are sick" (Matt. 9:12).

Do you recall the setting for those words of Jesus? Jesus was eating with tax collectors and sinners, and the Pharisees wanted to know why such a holy man would do this, risk such defilement. So Jesus answered them, "Go and learn what this means, 'I desire mercy, and not sacrifice.' For I came not to call the righteous, but sinners" (Matt. 9:13).

I spoke not long ago at an evangelism rally of the South Indiana Conference of the United Methodist Church. Bishop Ralph Alton was asked to welcome the people. He took what could have been a perfunctory task and made a prophetic proclamation. He shocked the audience by saying he was not sure he was happy they were there. He was not sure because too many people attend gatherings such as that to talk about evangelism and feel that in talking about it they had fulfilled their responsibility. He closed his remarks saying, "If you have come to talk about evangelism with no intention of doing evangelism when you return home, I'm sorry you've come. But, if you are here to talk and learn and pray in order to return and be about the task, welcome!"

The deadly perversion of hatred, the degenerate prostitution of power, and the distorted perception of religion—these are some relevant truths from a sweeping look at the scriptural setting of the claim of Jesus: "You say that I am a king."

Let's now look specifically at the claim. There are two words that help us in appropriating meaning: *abdication* and *coronation*.

Unless a king or a queen leaves the throne by death, he or she must abdicate before another can ascend the throne. We've had a few dramatic instances of that in history.

Now here is the idea as that relates to us. We occupy the throne of our lives. Our will is the seat of authority, and this is where we have to abdicate. To be a Christian is to will that Jesus be Lord of our lives.

Somewhere along the way I read a pamphlet entitled, "Annie Doesn't Live Here Anymore." It was the witness of a woman giving testimony to God's transforming power in her life. She had lived many years in sin, with no restraint on her passions and her deeds. She had played the field of sin. Then, by a miracle of God's grace, someone witnessed to her of the redeeming love of God and led her to accept Christ as her personal savior and commit her life to him. In the pamphlet, she described her life of sin with its problems and pain, its seaminess and sorrow. Then she showed how God delivered her from her old life and gave her a new life. Therefore, across the door of her old life, she had placed the sign, "Annie Doesn't Live Here

Anymore." That's what abdication means. We abdicate to Christ; we come down off the throne of our lives, accepting the forgiveness of Christ and willingly making him king.

That leads to the second word, *coronation*. Unlike any earthly model of kingship we know, Jesus is king only of those who choose him, only of those who will deliberately crown him Lord of their lives. No wonder Jesus said, "My kingship is not of this world."

Abdication is the beginning of Jesus' lordship in our lives. Coronation is the continuing process of making him Lord.

I began this chapter with mine and Jerry's experience of being in the presence of royalty. I close with a similar experience of a friend.

I went to college with a girl named Mary Bozeman. Mary made a decision in her last year of college to make Jesus king. She abdicated the throne of her life, accepted Christ as Savior, and sought to make her life a coronation of Jesus as Lord. I still vividly remember visiting Mary in Brussels, Belgium, when she was studying, making final preparations to go as a missionary to what was then the Belgian Congo. I think it was that experience, when I was a first-year student in seminary, that really fired my intense interest in missions.

In the other missionaries who were there, but especially in Mary, I saw something dynamic and challenging that I had not to that point experienced about the Christian faith. I have never witnessed a more vivid testimony of the presence of Christ within the life of an individual. Here was a young woman leaving home and friends, going to the wilds of what was then an almost unknown continent. It was a life commitment. What consecration! It radiated from her very countenance. There was an atmosphere that set her apart. And I know why. She gave the reason in a letter that we received from her.

> Only a few days after arriving here in Brussels they celebrated an independence day, much like our celebration of the Fourth of July. So I heard the king would lead the parade and I wanted to see him. I was told by several Belgian people I would have to get in place at least three hours ahead of time if I wanted to see the king. Well, believe me, this was hard going when I awakened this particular morning and saw a rainy, dismal dawn. Thank God for raincoats . . . I certainly made use of mine for three hours, standing on a street corner waiting for a glimpse of royalty. But I did see him, young, handsome, and single.
>
> This was the first king I had ever seen in person, but not the first king I had ever met. It was a thrilling experience to see the king of Belgium, but not the most thrilling. The most thrilling experience I've ever had was when I met the King of kings, and gave Him my life.

Mary knew. In a tone and spirit altogether different from his word to Pilate, Jesus would say to Mary, "You say that I am a king."

What would he say to you? In Luke's account of the events of this day, the Pharisees challenged Jesus for accepting the praise of the people. "Teacher, rebuke your disciples," they said. He answered them, "I tell you, if these were silent, the very stones would cry out" (Luke 19:39–40).

Whether we say so or not, Jesus is still king. If we fail to say so, even the rocks will cry out. Wouldn't it be tragic if a single person remained silent and left it to the stones to proclaim, "Hosanna to the king!"

Look at your life, your own relationship to Jesus. Can Jesus say to you affirmingly, tenderly, acceptingly, "You say that I am a king"?

6

I Am the Resurrection and the Life

Now Jesus loved Martha and her sister and Lazarus. So when he heard that he was ill, he stayed two days longer in the place where he was. Then after this he said to the disciples, "Let us go to Judea again." The disciples said to him, "Rabbi, the Jews were but now seeking to stone you, and are you going there again?" Jesus answered, "Are there not twelve hours in the day? If any one walks in the day, he does not stumble, because he sees the light of this world. But if any one walks in the night, he stumbles, because the light is not in him." Thus he spoke, and then he said to them, "Our friend Lazarus has fallen asleep, but I go to awake him out of sleep." The disciples said to him, "Lord, if he has fallen asleep, he will recover." Now Jesus had spoken of his death, but they thought that he meant taking rest in sleep. Then Jesus told them plainly, "Lazarus is dead; and for your sake I am glad that I was not there, so that you may believe. But let us go to him." Thomas, called the Twin, said to his fellow disciples, "Let us also go, that we may die with him."

Now when Jesus came, he found that Lazarus had already been in the tomb four days. Bethany was near Jerusalem, about two miles off, and many of the Jews had come to Martha and Mary to console them concerning their brother. When Martha heard that Jesus was coming, she went and met him, while Mary sat in the house. Martha said to Jesus, "Lord, if you had been here, my brother would not have died. And even now I know that whatever you ask from God, God will give you." Jesus said to her, "Your brother will rise again." Martha said to him, "I know that he will rise again in the resurrection at the last day." Jesus said to her, "I am the resurrection and the life; he who believes in me, though he die, yet shall he live, and whoever lives and believes in me shall never die. Do you believe this?" She said to him, "Yes, Lord; I believe that you are the Christ, the Son of God, he who is coming into the world."

—John 11:5–27

In *Learning to Say Good-by,* Eda LeShan tells of visiting a friend of hers who had lost her husband. They went to the cemetery and stood by the grave. There they shared some memories. Then they were silent. Nobody seemed to have anything to say. Then the young daughter in the family, a little girl named Liz, all of a sudden ran and did a cartwheel over the grave. Eda LeShan must have looked surprised because Liz's mother, smiling broadly, turned to her and said, "Liz hasn't done any cartwheels since Bob died. He used to love it when she did."

Reflecting upon this, LeShan said:

I tried to understand just what Liz's message to her father meant. Then I realized that her gift to him was to pick up the threads of her life and to begin to live as fully as she could. The time comes to begin

to do cartwheels again—to express our joy in being
alive.

I don't know what you feel about that story. I
don't know how I would have reacted in the moment had I been there and seen a little girl doing
cartwheels over her father's grave. But hearing the
story, and being able to think about it, I see it as an
Easter symbol.

The great claim of Jesus which we consider in
this chapter is one of his boldest: "I am the resurrection and the life." Rehearse the scriptural setting for this claim. It's a beautiful love story. Mary,
Martha, and their brother Lazarus are beloved
friends of Jesus. Luke is the only other gospel
writer who mentions Jesus' relationship with this
family, though Mark and Matthew tell us that, during Jesus' time in Jerusalem, he spent his evenings
in Bethany. We can confidently assume that it was
in the home of Mary, Martha, and Lazarus that
Jesus stayed. In keeping with his style of writing,
John gives us details and intimate observations.

It should not surprise us that John gave a very
prominent position in his Gospel to the raising of
Lazarus. John records events and details of Jesus'
ministry not found in the other Gospels: the inter-
view with the woman at the well, Nicodemus, the
wedding at Cana, the young man born blind, and
the man at the pool of Bethesda. According to
John, it is the Lazarus miracle that triggers the
wrath of Jesus' opponents and leads them to agree
to their deadly strategy against him.

Jesus is in Perea, across Jordan, when the
news comes to him of Lazarus. "This illness is not

unto death; it is for the glory of God, so that the Son of God may be glorified," said Jesus (John 11:4). He stays on for two days, then announces to his disciples that he is going to Bethany and Jerusalem. This upsets the disciples because they know the menace against Jesus has grown. Jesus tells them he is going to raise Lazarus from death "so that you may believe."

When they arrive in Bethany, Lazarus has been buried. Now comes the dramatic event. The practical sister, Martha comes out to meet Jesus; fragile, emotional Mary mourns in the house.

"Lord, if you had been here," Martha says to Jesus, "my brother would not have died." If she had stopped there it would reflect only disappointment and grief. But she moves on to make clear her confident faith. "And even now I know that whatever you ask from God, God will give you." Though strong and confident, it is doubtful if Martha realized the full meaning of what she said. Jesus tells her: "Your brother will rise again."

Again Martha expresses confidence in Jesus and a certain faith. Not knowing that Jesus is speaking of an *immediate* reality, she says, "I know that he will rise again in the resurrection at the last day." Martha's hope is in the future.

At this point comes Jesus' most moving of his great claims: "I am the resurrection and the life; he who believes in me, though he die, yet shall he live, and whoever lives and believes in me shall never die." This is no promise of some obscure, future hope, but victory over death now and eternal life in the present.

Let's register three powerful meanings in this claim of Jesus. One, because Jesus is the resurrection and the life, we can sustain a vision of hope. Two, all walls are vulnerable. And, three, we are not victims either of circumstances or death. Let's look at these meanings and in doing so discover our promises in Jesus' claims.

First, because Jesus is the resurrection and the life, we can sustain a vision of hope. Even before Jesus, God planted a vision of hope in the minds and hearts of his people. We see it dramatically in one chapter of the history of God's people. When Moses and Joshua were leading them out of captivity, and they came near the promised land, the Israelites were in the choking grip of negative thinking. They had a defeatist mentality and wallowed in their despair. They complained about everything. The food was not good, and the accommodations were worse. They were frightened of the future. They criticized Moses and Joshua, accusing them of a subversive plot to kill them. Day after day they moped around and complained. When they surveyed the land God had promised them, they laid on themselves the ultimate put-down—they saw themselves as grasshoppers and their enemies as giants.

Moses, their great leader, grew weary of their complaining antagonism. Joshua was fed up. Even God cried out, "How long shall this wicked congregation murmur against me?" (Num. 14:27). To add to the despair and hopelessness, Moses died.

Then an amazing thing happened. The first chapter of Joshua opens with this word:

> After the death of Moses the servant of the Lord, the Lord said to Joshua the son of Nun, Moses' minister, "Moses my servant is dead; now therefore arise, go over this Jordan, you and all this people, into the land which I am giving to them."
> —Joshua 1:1–2

For forty years Moses had been the leader. Joshua and the people of Israel had depended upon him. He was the great emancipator. Now he was dead, and the people and Joshua were discouraged and depressed. But God said, "Arise! Get up! Be done with this hopelessness; go over into Jordan, you and all the people, into the land which I am giving to them" (AP).

That fired hope. And you know the amazing thing that happened. This defeated, discouraged people were transformed. Though they were the descendants of slaves with no military training at all, fortified with faith and hope, they moved into a land occupied by people with vastly superior weapons and fortified cities, and they conquered it.

How did this happen? What was their secret? They took God at his promise. And what was that promise? Listen to Joshua 1:5–6:

> No man shall be able to stand before you all the days of your life; as I was with Moses, so I will be with you; I will not fail you or forsake you. Be strong and of good courage; for you shall cause this people to inherit the land which I swore to their fathers to give them.

I could have used any number of stories to dramatize the vision of hope which God planted in the minds and hearts of his people. But I used this one of Joshua because Jesus is our Joshua. *Joshua* is the Hebrew name for *Jesus*. Jesus is the fulfillment of the law of Moses, but more. As God allowed Joshua to enter the land of promise, Jesus leads us to the ultimate Promised Land.

Before the resurrection, hope was dependent upon the episodic breaking in of God upon human history. But now there is a once-and-for-all event. Because of the resurrection we can sustain a vision of hope. Hope has been given the substance of life itself. That's the reason Paul argued so forcefully in the fifteenth chapter of First Corinthians that the resurrection was the hinge issue of the Christian faith. "If Christ has not been raised, your faith is futile and you are still in your sins. . . . If for this life only we have hoped in Christ, we are of all men most to be pitied" (1 Cor. 15:17,19).

I think of Deborah Kerr during the making of the movie *Quo Vadis*. At one point in the picture she was tied to a stake in the Roman Coliseum. Angry lions are turned loose and rush at her. A reporter asked, "Weren't you afraid when those lions were loosed and came plunging at you?" She replied, "No, I am one of those actresses who reads *all* the script. I had read to the end and I knew Robert Taylor would come and save me."

Lift that to an infinitely higher level; read the biblical witness. "Hope" for the Christian is not hoping in the normal sense of that word; it is not wishful thinking. It is the very substance of faith which gives us our greatest certainty. I like that word from the epistle to the Hebrews: "But we are not of those who shrink back and are destroyed, but of those who have faith and keep their souls" (Heb. 10:39). No wonder we sing so joyfully that magnificent contemporary gospel hymn by William J. and Gloria Gaither which sounds the note so challengingly.

Because he lives I can face tomorrow;
Because he lives all fear is gone;
Because I know he holds the future,
And life is worth the living just because he lives.

Not only can we sustain a vision of hope, but because Jesus is the resurrection and the life, all walls are *vulnerable*. One of the most dramatic things that happened when Jesus was crucified was that the veil of the Temple was rent in twain from top to bottom. That veil was the veil which hid the holy of holies. It was the place wherein dwelt the very presence of God. Only one man, the high priest, could enter that place, and that only once a year, on the great Day of Atonement. The very spirit of God dwelt within that holy of holies. There is tremendous symbolism here. Until that time, God had been hidden and remote, and no one knew what God was like. But now, the heart of God, hitherto hidden, was laid bare to persons. In the death of Jesus, we see the hidden love of God. What happened on Golgotha at that particular time in history was going on in the heart of God from the very beginning. So, the way which was once closed to all humans is now open. All persons can come into the presence of God.

The coming of Jesus—the life of Jesus and the death of Jesus—rent the veil which had concealed

God from humankind. "He who has seen me," said Jesus, "has seen the Father" (John 14:9). On the cross, as never before and as will never happen again, we see the love of God. In the resurrection, the power of God prevails. In that event, God said, "No more! Never! Never again will you be separated from me." Because Jesus is the resurrection and the life, every wall is vulnerable.

It matters not what the walls are. It may be a wall

- between you and God, because you have sinned and fallen short of his glory. You have allowed sin to reign without being repentant and seeking forgiveness.
  A WALL IS THERE.

- between you and God because you have been dull to God's call, you have spurned his love, you have cried, "Lord, Lord," but have not done his will. You have not been obedient. You keep holding back in the giving of yourself, holding back in the tithe of your money, holding back in your witness.
  A WALL IS THERE.

It matters not what the walls are. It may be a wall

- between you and your spouse because you have allowed past hurt to go unacknowledged and unhealed. Those hurts have festered into a poisonous sore.
  A WALL IS THERE.

- between you and your spouse because one of you knows the unfaithfulness of the other, and there has not yet been any repentance, confession, and forgiveness.

A WALL IS THERE.

- between you and your spouse because one or both of you have allowed the fire of love to die. You haven't kept the flame kindled by giving and forgiving, by caring, by all those acts of tenderness and agape love, self-giving for the sake of others.

A WALL IS THERE.

It matters not what the walls are. It may be a wall

- between you and one of your children. You've grown weary in giving and giving and giving, and the uncaring response of your child has worn you down to the point of despair.

A WALL IS THERE.

- between you and a child who is even more separated, the child who is in the far country and is spending his or her life in riotous living. Your heart is broken, the pain is well nigh unbearable.

A WALL IS THERE.

And, young people, you may feel the walls too:

- between you and your parents. You feel they don't understand, that they don't even try to understand, that they are more interested in your performance than they are in you as a person. They don't listen.

A WALL IS THERE.

- between you and your friends. You try to live
  the faith. You want to be a Christian, but to
  them that doesn't make sense. They want
  you "cool" like you once were.
  A WALL IS THERE.

The catalogue could go on and on. You know,
because walls are real. But this is the good news:
Because Christ is the resurrection and the life, all
walls are vulnerable. There is no wall that he can't
penetrate and dissolve. Before his love and forgiveness, and the power he gives us to love and
forgive, all walls may be broken down.

Because Jesus is the resurrection and the life,
we can sustain a vision of hope, and all walls are
vulnerable. Now, perhaps the greatest truth of all:
Because Jesus is the resurrection and the life, we
are not *victims,* either of circumstance or of death.
We are victors.

Huber Matos was a teacher and a journalist
who was imprisoned by Castro in 1959 when Castro sought to destroy the church in Cuba. Many
Christian leaders and those who courageously
stood for freedom were imprisoned. In a letter
smuggled out of a Havana prison, a letter to his wife
and children, Matos said, "I know that I will die in
prison. I am sad not to see you again, but I am at
peace. They have swords, but we have songs."

See the difference between Matos and an attractive young woman of whom I read. She was
intelligent and fabulously wealthy. With energy and
shrewdness, she had amassed a fortune in the
world of investments. She seemed to have it all, but

she was lacking something, like the rich young ruler who went to Jesus because of his inner emptiness. The young woman drove her silver Mercedes convertible to a hotel, checked in, and then checked out for good. She died of a drug overdose, leaving a note that read: "I'm tired of clapping with one hand."

That young woman did not know the peace, she did not have the song of Matos. She did not know Jesus who is the resurrection and the life. She did not know this One who always lives to make intercession for us (Heb. 7:25).

Because Jesus is the resurrection and the life, we are not victims of circumstance. We don't have to clap with one hand. Nor are we victims of death. Dr. Raymond E. Balcomb, a Methodist minister in Oregon, tells a story that illustrates the truth.

An eleven-year-old boy was dying of an incurable disease. He was an only child; his parents had sought out one specialist after another, but none had been able to help. The mother had become reconciled to the inevitable, but the father was bitter and unaccepting. It was Christmas Eve and the father couldn't sleep. He tossed and turned, and finally went out to the living room. Under the Christmas tree were a lot of presents the boy would be able to use very little, if at all—a football, some games, a chemistry set. As he pondered the cruel injustice of it all, he gradually began to pray.

Dear God, (he began) something has happened. I ask you to hear me out. As I sit here, I remember what a personal success I have been and how you have responded whenever I asked you to give me a hand. But I know now those were selfish prayers for my own personal gain. And when I asked you to save Billy, that was personal and selfish, too. I couldn't stand to lose him. I had such great plans for him, and I wanted someday for him to carry on for me. I wanted everybody to know what a fine boy I had raised.

Father, you know what I remember now? I remember your son and your great love when you gave him to the world. What sadness you must have felt when he died! And so God, if you would do this one thing for all of us, then I have to be comforted by your sacrifice. It's a long time since I put my full trust in you. So I pray now that you will welcome Billy when he comes. I know he will be in good hands. Thy will be done.

It was almost time for Billy's medication, so he went in to give it to him. The boy was awake, took his dad's hand and said, "Dad, I won't need those pills tonight." The father asked why not. "I've been dreaming, Dad. I've been dreaming about Jesus. He seemed very close. It sounds funny, but it's almost as though he's here in this room with us right now." And his hand relaxed its grip on his father's, his eyes closed, and the last breath of life went from him with a gentle sigh.

He went home. Neither he nor his father were the victims of circumstances or death; they were the victors.

Because Jesus is the resurrection and the life, we can sustain a *vision* of hope; all walls are *vul-*

nerable; and we are not *victims* of circumstance or even death.

Go back to my beginning story. The little girl, Liz, acted out her faith by doing a cartwheel over her father's grave. What do you suppose the angels in heaven did at the resurrection of Jesus? Might they have done cartwheels of joy? What should be our response? At least a shout of "Hallelujah!" for the Lord Christ reigns, King of kings and Lord of lords.

7

I Am the Alpha and the Omega

The revelation of Jesus Christ, which God gave him to show to his servants what must soon take place; and he made it known by sending his angel to his servant John, who bore witness to the word of God and to the testimony of Jesus Christ, even to all that he saw. Blessed is he who reads aloud the words of the prophecy, and blessed are those who hear, and who keep what is written therein; for the time is near.

John to the seven churches that are in Asia:
Grace to you and peace from him who is and who was and who is to come, and from the seven spirits who are before his throne, and from Jesus Christ the faithful witness, the first-born of the dead, and the ruler of kings of earth.
To him who loves us and has freed us from our sins by his blood and made us a kingdom, priests to his God and Father, to him be glory and dominion for ever and ever. Amen. Behold, he is coming with the clouds, and every eye will see him, every one who pierced him; and all tribes of the earth will wail on account of him. Even so. Amen.
"I am the Alpha and the Omega," says the

Lord God, who is and who was and who is to come, the Almighty.

—Revelation 1:1–8

Many of you know the name Lloyd C. Douglas, author of *The Robe* and other novels. It has been reported that when Douglas was a university student, he lived in a boarding house. Downstairs on the first floor was an elderly, retired music teacher, now infirm and unable to leave the apartment. Douglas said that every morning they had a ritual that they would go through together. He would come down the steps, open the old man's door and ask, "Well, what's the good news?" The old man would pick up his tuning fork, tap it on the side of his wheelchair and say, "That's middle C! It was middle C yesterday; it will be middle C tomorrow; it will be middle C a thousand years from now. The tenor upstairs sings flat, the piano across the hall is out of tune, but, my friend, that is middle C!"

The old man had discovered one thing upon which he could depend, one constant reality in his life, one "still point in a turning world." For Christians, the one "still point in a turning world," the one absolute of which there is no shadow of turning, is Jesus Christ. We've been considering his own claims about himself. We come now to that climactic claim. It is the word of revelation given to John on the isle of Patmos, a word of finality and hope. "I am the Alpha and the Omega, [the One] who is and who was and who is to come."

The words *alpha* and *omega* denote the first and last letters of the Greek alphabet, so we might translate this word "I am the *A* and the *Z*."

Get the setting for the claim in mind. Jesus is speaking to John on the isle of Patmos. John, now an old man, is in exile. The church is under severe persecution. Terror and evil reign. John has probably been exiled because he refused to worship the emperor.

The Book of Revelation comes from this exile. It's a very difficult book to understand, and many commentators have handled it altogether too casually. To even begin to read it, you have to know that it is the most poetic book in the Bible; it abounds in symbols, symbols that are completely foreign to us. It is what we call *apocalyptic* literature, and according to Earl F. Palmer in *The Communicator's Commentary:*

> The nature of apocalyptic literature is distinguished by the threefold mixture of hiddenness, of vast upheaval, and of decisive divine act. There is often a heavy pessimism on one page, which is then surprised by the sudden breakthrough of God's mighty act on the next page. These are marks of apocalyptic writing.

The Book of Revelation may be called *prophetic,* though not nearly as much as *apocalyptic.* Again, Earl Palmer's insights are helpful:

> Prophetic writing is even more common in the Jewish and Christian tradition than is the apocalyptic. The largest part of the Old Testament prophets is prophetic writing. Such writing, which is theological, evangelistic, and ethical by nature, intends to call people to repentance. The prophetic message emphasizes the decision-making freedom of the people before God, whereas the apocalyptic mes-

sage emphasizes the freedom of God. Prophetic preaching calls out and affirms the implications of the will of God to the people here and now and, therefore, has a more present tense cutting edge; its meaning is not as mysterious and hidden as in the apocalyptic. The mark of the prophetic word is its clarity and its immediacy.

So we are looking at apocalyptic literature primarily, with hidden meaning and veiled symbols, but such literature would be familiar to the people of the first century.

As John sat alone, perhaps in a cave on the isle of Patmos, he felt helpless, removed from the heat of conflict. His heart was broken over the persecution of the church. Waiting and wondering, pictures of persons whom he had won to Christ flashed on the screen of his mind, and the pain in his heart grew sharper. Worried and uncertain, questions began to play havoc with his faith.

There were times when his reflections were pervaded with joy. He remembered the excitement of following Jesus, the excruciating pain and despair of the crucifixion, the exhilarating victory of the resurrection, the miracles that followed the infilling power of the Holy Spirit at Pentecost. The church was imbued with the Spirit which brought power. John himself had won thousands to believe in the gospel. But now, here he was, worrying and wondering, but keeping faith alive by prayer and memory.

Then came his revelation. He was "in the Spirit on the Lord's day" (Rev. 1:10). The vision came like the brilliant sun breaking through a stormy sky, and the voice was like a trumpet: "I am the Alpha and the Omega . . . the beginning and the end" (Rev. 22:13).

Before him stood the Son of man himself, majestic, immense. In *Over His Own Signature,* Leslie D. Weatherhead imagines the scene:

> The paling stars seemed at his fingertips. The woolly, fleecy clouds at the zenith seemed to crown him with a supernatural purity. His eyes were flames of fire and his feet caught the yellow glory of the sunrise and shone like burnished brass. His countenance was radiant with sunshine and his voice mingled with the crashing breakers in front of him. John fell prostrate on the beach. His depression had vanished. He was "in the Spirit on the Lord's day," as truly as if he had been in his beloved temple at Jerusalem, and his Master was as near to him. He seemed to feel a touch on his shoulder and that voice like many waters spoke the old familiar words which Jesus had used so often: "Fear not!"
>
> Breathless now with adoration, John listened as the beloved inner Voice continued: "Fear not; I am the first and the last, and the Living One; and I was dead, and behold, I am alive for evermore, and I have the keys of death and of Hades." (Revelation 1:17–18)

That is the middle C of the Christian faith. John came back to repeat it as he closed his record of his revelation, chapter 22, verse 13: "I am the Alpha and the Omega, the first and the last, the beginning and the end."

Like all the great "I am" claims of Jesus, this one is fathomless in its meaning—maybe more so than any of the others. It is a heightened crescendo of affirmation, crowning all the other claims with a finality and a completeness that we need to consider. So we look at it humbly, knowing that if we touch just the hem of the garment of its meaning, the Lord will honor our faith and finish his work in us.

Center on the two big claims Jesus makes in the one claim: "I am the *beginning* and [I am] the *end*" or *completion*. Jesus is the beginning of life and love, and he is the ending or completion of history. First, Jesus is the beginning of life. John stated it clearly in his prologue to the Gospel.

> In the beginning was the Word, and the Word was with God, and the Word was God. He was in the beginning with God; all things were made through him, and without him was not anything made that was made. In him was life, and the life was the light of men. The light shines in the darkness, and the darkness has not overcome it.
> —John 1:1–5

We don't stop often enough and reflect deeply enough about who this Christ is. Jesus is not just a good man, not even the best of all men, not just a mighty prophet among prophets, not just one god in a lineup of deities from whom we may choose. All things were made by him. In him was life. He is the beginning of the created order. He is the preexistent Christ. He is the cosmic Christ. No glory belongs to God that does not belong to Jesus Christ.

But not only life itself—being, existing—not only is Jesus the beginning of our just being alive, he is the beginning of our new life, our being alive to God. Consider again John's response to Christ:

When I saw him, I fell at his feet as though dead.
But he laid his right hand upon me, saying, "Fear
not, I am the first and the last, and the living one; I
died, and behold I am alive for evermore, and I
have the keys of Death and Hades."
                                —Revelation 1:17–18

Sense the power of that. Calvary and Easter are
held together in tandem: "I died, and behold I am
alive for evermore."

The cross is always basic; it brings us back to
the source of our new life. The sacrifice of Golgotha
is our confidence that we are forgiven, that though
our sins make us scarlet, we shall be as white as
snow; and as far as the East is from the West, just
that far will he remove our sins from us. *He died,*
and so we are freed of any illusion that we have to
be anything or *do* anything in order to be loved and
accepted of God.

He died, but more. "I am alive for evermore,"
Jesus said. "I have the keys of Death and Hades."
The confirmation of new life is here in the resurrection: Jesus is alive for evermore, and we have his
promise, "Because I live, you will live also" (John
14:19).

Christ is the beginning of life, but also *the beginning of love*. Consider John's benediction upon
the Christians to whom he was writing—"To him
who loves us and has freed us from our sins by his
blood and made us a kingdom, priests to his God
and father, to him be glory and dominion for ever
and ever."

When I say Jesus is the beginning of love, I
mean that until Jesus came, the love of God was
never perceived fully. Oh, there were great break-

throughs in human experience. Hosea knew God's heart and quoted God, saying, "When Israel was a child, I loved him, and out of Egypt I called my son. . . . I led them with cords of compassion, with the bands of love" (Hos. 11:1,4).

Micah saw it, too:

Who is a God like thee, pardoning iniquity,
and passing over transgression
for the remnant of his inheritance?
He does not retain his anger for ever
because he delights in steadfast love.
He will again have compassion on us,
he will tread our iniquities under foot.
Thou wilt cast all our sins
into the depths of the sea.
—Micah 7:18–19

But now, it is revealed fully. Let it penetrate the depths of our beings; let it be imprinted indelibly upon our consciousness—*unto him who loves us*. How and to what end? By the blood of love on the cross, he has freed us from our sins and has made us a kingdom of priests with free access to the father forever and ever. No wonder John calls for praise: "To him be glory and dominion for ever and ever." Jesus Christ is the beginning of life and love.

Christ is the beginning of life, but also the ending or the completion—the ending or completion of history.

We have to talk now about the Second Coming. Unfortunately, in most of our so-called mainline churches, we don't talk enough about the Second Coming. There is a vacuum in thought and conviction, and thus people are left to all sorts of confused and distorted notions.

Too many people argue about the Second Coming. Instead of arguing, let's affirm. My conviction is with the two ancient creeds of the church, the Nicene and Apostles'. The Nicene Creed (much like the Apostles' Creed) states that Christ "ascended into heaven, and sitteth at the right hand of the Father; and he shall come again with glory, to judge both the quick and the dead; whose kingdom shall have no end." Behind the creed is the gospel of the New Testament. According to D. T. Niles in *A Testament of Faith*:

> While men can enact the cross, they cannot prevent the resurrection. He is Lord. The New Testament faith carries forward this assertion of Christ's present sovereignty into the further assertion that He will come again. He came once in humiliation. He will come again in glory. He came the first time to initiate. He will come again to consummate. When He came in the flesh, He came to share man's life, to suffer for him and to die. When He comes again as risen and ascended Lord, He will come to bring the human story to its end. He will come to judge.

Let me now make a few assertions which I think are important as we think about the Second Coming.

First, no one knows when the Second Coming is going to be. Jesus himself said that. "Watch then," he said, "because you do not know the day or the hour" (Matt. 24:42, AP).

Second, there is not a clear picture in the scripture for the nature of Christ's earthly rule. Some committed Christians believe that there will be a spiritual rule of Christ on earth for a thousand years before the final judgment; others, equally committed, believe that the thousand-year rule on earth will follow his Second Coming. Still others believe that his kingdom will be established on earth, so the thousand-year reign is not an issue. Some Christians believe in a rapture and some do not, and both have scriptural support. So there is not a clear scriptural picture of Christ's earthly rule.

Third, to try to reduce the message of scripture to the motif of prophecy and fulfillment is, I believe, at best an extremely limited approach to scripture, and at worst, an abomination of God's word.

There is some apocalyptic and so-called prophecy teaching that is totally devoid of a focus on Christ. In this teaching, the story of Jesus the Messiah becomes simply a part of the demonstration of the accuracy of biblical prophecy. The result is that the significance of the death and resurrection of Christ in the determination of the future for which Christians hope is unclear. Therefore, speculation about the final events of history and the return of Jesus the Messiah runs rampant. (See J. Christiaan Beker, *Paul's Apocalyptic Gospel*, p. 27 and following.)

Now, having affirmed that, let me lodge two words in your mind that will help us think clearly about the Second Coming. Those words are *vindication* and *validation*.

Vindication means judgment. Christ is going to judge the living and the dead. "I have the keys of

Death and Hades," Christ said to John. This is a matter of salvation and damnation, and it must never be diminished. You and I will be judged, and Christ's judgment of us will determine whether we die eternally, cast into outer darkness where, as the scripture says, there will be weeping and wailing and gnashing of teeth (Matt. 13:42), or whether we will live eternally, enjoying the presence of the Lord, and the rewards of his glory.

But there is a second word: the validation of God's love and faithfulness. Validation is the positive expression of God's judgment. Jesus is the source of this validation. Paul proclaims it in Second Corinthians 1:20: "For all the promises of God find their Yes in him [Christ]." That is why we utter the amen through him, to the glory of God.

The validation of which I speak is the validation of God's faithfulness, not the restoration of a modern state of Israel, which is the dominant teaching of so many who are emphasizing prophecy and the Second Coming today. It is the validation of God's faithfulness in the establishment of God's kingdom. John's vision was that there will be a new heaven and a new earth. The lion will lie down with the lamb. *Shalom* will be the spirit of the kingdom because swords will be beaten into plowshares and spears into pruning hooks. There will be no more war. Neither will there be any more sorrow or pain or death or separation. All will be wholeness and life for Jesus, the Healer and Redeemer will reign. His kingdom will know no end and his joy will be complete.

In light of this, the question is, "How then shall we live?" We are not called to try to figure out when the end will come. We are not called to try to figure out all the technicolor images and symbols which fill the pages of Daniel and Revelation. We are not called to determine who will be in and who will be out.

We are called to be at our task, the task of being faithful to the work God has given us to do, to be a part of the work of God's kingdom, and to continue to pray, as we work, that God's kingdom will come on earth as it is in heaven.

There is one sure way of judging the integrity of any teaching about prophecy. Does it have a clear ethical content, a clear call to righteousness and holiness? So much so-called *prophecy* that we hear today is bereft of the *prophetic*. The emphasis is upon prediction, not performance. Not so with the Bible. The concern is not with *when* the Son of man is going to return, but what he will find us doing when he returns.

The message is consistent throughout every one of Jesus' parables and stories about the final coming. The pattern is much the same in every one. An example of it is the parable of the master who put his servants in charge of his property when he went on a trip. He came back to check things out and the servants who had been faithful to their trust, who had used what they were given wisely and well, were rewarded. But the ones who had abused their master's trust and squandered their gifts were cast out. Jesus closed that parable saying, "Happy is the servant who is found at his task when his Master comes" (Luke 12:43, AP).

If Jesus comes today or tomorrow or next week, the question will not simply be, "Are you ready?" in the sense of "Have you believed and trusted Christ for your salvation?" That is certainly crucial: no one is taken to glory except those whose lives have been cleansed by the blood of the Lamb. But the returning Christ will expect *validation* of our cleansing and commitment. So the big question is: "What will he find us doing when he comes?"

> Will he find us
> > witnessing to his saving grace to our neighbors, friends, and colleagues?

> Will he find us
> > actively engaged in protesting all that which profanes and limits life?

> Will he find us
> > making peace in every way possible?

> Will he find us
> > doing that which he said would be the criteria by which we would be judged "sheep" or "goats," that is,
> > > feeding the hungry,
> > > clothing the naked,
> > > caring for the prisoners,
> > > visiting the sick?

There was a Negro slave who discovered the right perspective and put it in these words:

> There's a king and captain high,
> And he's coming bye and bye,
> And he'll find me hoeing cotton
> > when he comes.

You can hear his legions
Charging in the regions
Of the sky,
And he'll find me hoeing cotton
     when he comes.

There's a man they thrust aside,
Who was scorned and crucified,
And he'll find me hoeing cotton
     when he comes.

When he comes! When he comes!
He'll be crowned by saints and angels
When he comes.

They'll be shouting out Hosanna!
To the man that men denied,
And I'll kneel among my cotton
     when he comes.

May it be so for us, for the One whom we are called to love and serve is the Alpha and Omega, our beginning and our ending. He has the keys to life and death.

Study Questions

An Introductory Word

As you come together as a group, it will be helpful to agree on some ground rules for sharing and also to make some basic commitments.

Commitments:

- Attend all group meetings.
- Read the designated chapter and consider the questions related to it before the meeting.
- Pray daily for members of your group.

Ground rules:

- Agree on how long each meeting is to last and stick to the time.
- Make corporate prayer a part of each gathering.
- Give every person in the group an opportunity to share in each session. Guard against some persons talking too much and some too little.
- What is going on in persons' lives is more important than the content of the book.

> Allow the Spirit to use content to bring persons to share their own personal experience.
> - Cultivate a mood of concern that is marked by nonjudgment listening and genuine caring.
> - Allow the group sharing to be the springboard for the cultivation of ongoing relationships and daily concern for one another.

Chapter 1: **I Am the Bread of Life**

1. In a small group of two or three, share ways in which you have experienced the reality of Jesus' claim, "I am the bread of life," in a personal way. How has Jesus been the bread of life for you?

2. In John 6:26, Jesus accuses the people of wanting to be with him because he had fed them, not because they believed he was the son of God. Is it possible that we, too, follow Jesus out of a desire to enjoy the material rather than the spiritual benefits of being a Christian? Within your group, discuss examples from your own experience where this may be true.

3. Augustine said, "Without God, we cannot; without us, God will not." Discuss what you think he meant. Do you agree or disagree? Why?

4. If you had two loaves and sold one to buy lilies, what would you buy? Make a list of the five things you consider to be "lilies" in your life; then number them from the most important to the least important. Share your list with the members of your group.

5. Read together Matthew 4:4. In what ways are we tempted to give more importance to our physical lives than to our spiritual lives? List five things you do to care for yourself physically; then list five things you do to care for yourself spiritually. Share your lists with the group.

Chapter 2: **I Am the Good Shepherd**

1. Read aloud the images of the Good Shepherd from scripture (page 32). In what ways have you experienced Jesus as the Good Shepherd personally? Share one of these experiences with the group.

2. Take a few moments to reflect in silence upon the phrase, "Christ the Good Shepherd knows me—he knows my name." Allow the statement to sink deep into your awareness. Then choose a word that symbolizes for you your emotional reaction to that truth. Share that word with your group.

3. In what ways have you grown under the nurture of the Good Shepherd? In what ways do you

need to continue to grow? Share an example or two from each of these categories with your group if you are comfortable doing so.

4. What is it that you fear most in your life? Give a name to your fear and share that name with your group. Share only as much as you are comfortable sharing. When everyone has had an opportunity to share, pray for one another, calling upon the protection of Jesus, the Good Shepherd, against all fears.

5. The Good Shepherd protects us if we listen for and know his voice, and if we obey his voice when we hear it. Share in your group some of the ways in which you listen for Jesus' voice. How do you recognize his voice? What does Jesus ask of you that is easy for you to obey? What is hard for you to obey?

Chapter 3: **I Am the Door**

1. Take a few minutes to reflect upon the image of Jesus as the door. What is it that you would like Jesus to close behind you at this particular time in your life? If you would like to do so, share your desire with your group. When all have shared who wish to do so, gather in prayer for one another. Remember those desires expressed in the silence of the heart in your group prayer.

2. Read John 10:10 together. Jesus is not only the door that closes off our sin and guilt, our loss

and pain, he is the door that opens to a more abundant life. Share with the members of your group one of the most important ways in which Jesus has opened the door to a more abundant life for you.

3. In what way has the trustful relationship between you and God been experienced as a blessing; in what way has that relationship been tested; how has it been a source of strength for you on your spiritual journey?

4. Sometimes we become spiritually nearsighted and see Jesus as a door leading only one way, inward toward ourselves. But Jesus is the door that also leads outward, toward others. Take a few moments to reflect upon your own spiritual life. Is it balanced between its inner and outer dimensions. Does it lean toward the inner life? Is it focused more toward the outer life? Share your reflections with the others in your group.

5. Discuss needs you see crying out for loving service in your congregation, your community, your nation, the world. In what ways could you be Jesus' channel for meeting those needs? Share one commitment with your group that you are willing to make in loving service.

Chapter 4: **I Am the True Vine**

1. Reflect upon these statements for a few moments in silence; then share your responses with your group.

Jesus is most present to me in prayer when

_____.

I have difficulty being aware of Jesus' presence in prayer when _____.

Jesus is most present to me in scripture when

_____.

I have difficulty being aware of Jesus' presence in scripture when _____.

Jesus is most present to me in worship when

_____.

I have difficulty being aware of Jesus' presence in worship when _____.

2. There are many things to which Christians become attached instead of abiding in the True Vine. What are some of the things that tempt you most—security? success? popularity? What can you do to remove these things from the center of your life and abide in Christ?

3. Share with your group one time when you clearly experienced the probing or prodding of Christ. By what means did it come—through preaching, through a friend, through another person? How did you respond to it then? How do you feel about it now? What was the outcome?

4. Share the answers to the following questions with your group:

   At what moment this past week did you feel closest to Christ?

   At what moment during this week did you feel you were responding to God's call to be God's disciple?

   When was your faith tested this week through failure or by a great demand being made of you?

5. When did you most clearly experience being apart from Christ? What were the circumstances? What was your response to the situation? How was it resolved?

Chapter 5: **You Say That I Am a King**

1. Within your group, share the evidences of hatred and its poison that are visible in your day-to-day lives. Be aware of the subtle ways in which hatred works, and see if you can list five consequences of hatred within your own congregation, family, or community. Pray together as a group that the situations on your list may be transformed by the love of Christ.

2. The misuse of power is easy to recognize when it happens on a communitywide, nationwide, or

worldwide scale. However, it is not as recognizable when it occurs in our own lives and in the lives of our families. Share a personal experience of the misuse of power with your group. What ways are available to Christians to help them use power according to the sacrificial example of Jesus Christ?

3. With your group, make a list of the five characteristics of "religious" people that offend you the most. Then make a list of the five characteristics of Jesus that inspire you the most. Compare the two lists and discuss the differences between the two. What do you think accounts for these differences?

4. Take a few minutes to reflect in silence on your own spiritual journey. In what ways have you given Jesus Christ the kingship of your life; in what ways have you reserved that kingship for yourself? Share your reflections so far as you are comfortable with your group.

5. After you have completed your sharing as a group, pray with one another that the lordship of Jesus Christ will be a continuing reality in your lives.

Chapter 6: **I Am the Resurrection and the Life**

1. Share with your group a personal experience in which hope transformed defeat or despair into

victory. How did your hope sustain you; how was this a resurrection experience for you?

2. *Hoping* from the Christian perspective is much more than wishful thinking. Within your group, discuss the differences you see between the two. What accounts for those differences? Do Christians sometimes fall prey to wishful thinking rather than experiencing authentic hope; why or why not?

3. Take a few moments to reflect in silence upon the walls that may exist in your life between yourself and God. Try to identify those walls, whatever they may be for you. Choose a word or words that symbolize those walls for you. If you are comfortable doing so, share your word symbols with your group. After everyone has shared who wishes to share, pray together that your walls may prove vulnerable through Jesus' claim to be the resurrection and the life.

4. In what area of your life do you feel like a victim of circumstances—perhaps in a personal relationship, in your family, in your career? It may be an illness, great pain, or an unbearable sorrow. As a group, read aloud John 11:5–27. Take a few moments of silent reflection and affirm Jesus' claim to be the resurrection and the life as your personal promise in this situation.

5. Sharing within your group, take turns responding to the following statements:

In my spiritual journey, the thing that inspires hope in me most is _____.

The time I experienced resurrection most clearly was _____.

I am most vulnerable to new life in Christ when _____.

Chapter 7: **I Am the Alpha and the Omega**

1. Share with your group the way in which Jesus was the beginning of life for you. What were the circumstances of your conversion; how did you feel about the lordship of Christ at that point; how do you feel about it now?

2. Take a few moments to reflect upon the moment you first realized that Jesus loved you personally. Try to recapture the emotions of that experience vividly. How has that realization of Jesus' love changed you? Share that experience with your group.

3. Share with your group your beliefs about the Second Coming of Christ. How do your views differ; how are they similar? What are the most important implications of the Second Coming of Christ for you? Why?

4. Turn to page 113 and reflect for a few moments in silence upon the author's questions. Try to an-

swer honestly for yourself what Christ will find you doing when he comes. If you choose, share your reflections with your group.

5. Which "I am" claim of Jesus is the most real to you in your spiritual journey at this time? Why? Share your choice with your group.

Maxie Dunnam has served United Methodist churches in Georgia, Mississippi, California, and Tennessee. Prior to becoming Senior Minister of Christ United Methodist Church in Memphis, he was World Editor of The Upper Room.

Dr. Dunnam has published widely, including the popular three-book series: *The Workbook of Living Prayer, The Workbook of Intercessory Prayer,* and *The Workbook on Spiritual Disciplines.*

Dr. Dunnam and his wife Jerry have three children.